TIME AND TIDE

the story of Sheringham's fishermen and their families

Alan Childs and Ashley Sampson

MP

Time and Tide

the story of Sheringham's fishermen and their families

First published in 2004 by
Mousehold Press
Victoria Cottage
Constitution Opening
Norwich, NR3 4BD

Printed by Barnwells, Aylsham, Norfolk

ISBN 1 874739 32 3

Front cover photograph is of Bob 'Rally' West, Teddy 'Fiddy' West and Teddy's dog, Tim. It was said of the dog, 'If Teddy didn't take it, that swam after him.'

Back cover photograph of the Emery workshop shows Reg Emery (left) and his two sons, Harold (lower) and Chris.

To Jean and Sarah, for their support and patience over many months

Acknowledgements

Sources

It is with grateful thanks that we use extracts from recorded tapes, and quotations from written sources, indicated in the text by the following numbers:
1. Henry West; 2. Vera Childs; 3. May Ayers; 4. Anne and Lenny West; 5. Hazel Cheney; 6. Hazel Makins; 7. Reg Emery (from the BBC programme 'Down to the Sea', 1953); 8. Alan Forsdick; 9. Joe Pegg; 10. *The Motor Boat* (25 April 1924); 11. Henry Longhurst; 12. Brian Pegg; 13. Lenny West; 14. Bennett Middleton; 15. Bill Thirtle; 16. John Dennis; 17. Mollie West; 18. *Charlotte Upcher's Diary*; 19. Robert Long; 20. Jimmy West; 21. Clive Rayment; 22. Chris Ayers; 23. 'Coaly' Cooper; 24. Eastern Counties News-papers; 25. Henry Grice; 26. William Middleton; 27. Bob Rushmer; 28. Madge Gaff; 29. W. Shacklock; 30. Helen Richmond; 31. Geoff Storey; 32. Tony Sadler; 33. Teddy Craske.

Photographs

Sheringham Museum's own photographic collection has provided many of the images in this book. In addition, we have made use of photographs kindly offered to us by: Peter Brooks; Vera Childs; Stanley Craske Collection; Roy Cranmer; Jonathan Emery; Mike Emery; Malcolm Felmingham; Alan Forsdick; Madge Gaff; Margaret Goffin; Joy Harvey; Martyn Jackson; Rita McKenzie; Hazel Makins; David Mann; Cyril Nunn; Tony Sadler; Bill Thirtle; Lenny West.

We are grateful to the *Eastern Daily Press* and Aerofilms Ltd. who have kindly given us permission to use their photographs. Other photographers are: E. F. Bateman (p. 34, top); Alan Childs (p. 43 and p. 60, bottom); Geoffrey Clack (p. 29 top); Andrew Dawson (p. 83); Olive Edis (p. 14, top, p. 15, p. 17, both, p. 34, bottom, p. 46, p. 66); Tony Sadler (p. 52, bottom, and p. 76); Ashley Sampson (p. 58); C. Saul (p. 50); Harry Tansley (p. 18, p. 19. both, p. 22, p. 23, bottom, p. 36, p. 48, p. 49, top); Bill Thirtle (p. 81, top); Peter Villiers (p. 77, bottom).

Because of the age of many of the other photographs it has not been possible to identify the photographers.

Additional help

We are indebted to David Craske, Roy Craske, Deidre Crowfoot, Joy Hollingworth, Mark Makins, Mike Slipper, Chris Taylor and Olga Ward for all their help and support. We also wish to thank John Lown for permission to use a short extract from *Memories of Old Sheringham*, published by Sheringham History Group, 2003.

Our very sincere thanks to all those listed above, and particularly to Henry, Brian, Lenny and Bill, our four unfailing sources of fishing knowledge and who, together with Tony, Geoff, Malcolm and Roy, also kindly acted as readers. Our grateful thanks also to Adrian Bell of Mousehold Press, whose enthusiasm and support from the beginning carried this project forward.

We are also most grateful for the sponsorship of 'Tradewinds', suppliers of crabs and lobsters, and chandlery to the Industry (Mr and Mrs J. Lingwood), and of Stratton Long Marine, Blakeney.

FOREWORD

Over the years we have both seen many changes. The first notable change was from the rowing and sailing boats we can just remember, to the powered boats. The next big change was when the electric winch arrived. No longer were we heaving the boats up by hand-winch. It was time-saving, and labour-saving. There was also the change of gear from manilla and sisal, which you had to treat with ponica and tar, to man-made nylon and polypropylene, which are rot-proof. Now the pots are often left there from when they set them. A labour-saving device fitted to boats was the 'hauler'. When the later, and more suitable, diesel engines were installed, a hydraulic hauler was used. Before this, you had to work on the tides.

Over the years the boats got heavier and heavier. You would have to run them down on rollers and skeets to the water's edge. When fibreglass come on the scene, the boat industry moved from Sheringham. Boats are now smaller and lighter, more powerful, with the outboard engine, easier for one man working a boat. And fishing practically goes round the whole year now. Of course communication is another big change, now they've got mobile phones! When *we* first went to sea there was no means of letting people know if you was alright. But the fishing has declined, and the boats you can almost count on one hand. Even in our young times there were forty or fifty.

There's one thing that never changes and that's the sea. You still have to be careful, and the weather can be hard. It *is* dangerous if you don't know what you're doing. The sea got some people a good living all their lives, but they were very careful. They didn't take no chances. People don't understand how bad that can get. Over the years the people lost have been good fishermen. Anybody can get caught out. Look at the boards in the *Ramey Upcher* boat-shed.

Times were very hard in our early years, and harder still years ago. We were hard up and didn't have a penny. Some didn't know where the next penny was coming from – not just fishermen. But they were happy days, really. We shared so much – communal living. Baths used to hang on the wall and the toilet was on the opposite side. Lots of the fishermen were either Chapel or Salvation Army, but nearly all of them were God-fearing men. They wouldn't do nobody any harm, but they didn't all go to church and sit there Sunday after Sunday.

It was all team-work, helping one another, getting the boats down, and retrieving them. The same team-work goes into lifeboats. Both of us did 40 years in the lifeboat service, and we would do the same again, with the same people we crewed with. You learn as you go along, and from the word go we had a lot of trained people – been to sea all their lives. We've had sad times and we've had happy times. That's all part and parcel of lifeboat work. But it was a vocation. They were there doing the extra jobs because they were dedicated to saving life at sea. You *lived* fishing and lifeboats, hand in hand, one with the other. And that helped in more ways than one. And if you missed a trip, you were down. If it was rough, that was worse!

We have been pleased to help as much as we could with this book, to tell our experiences and the little bits we've linked to the past. We are happy to present it to the public as the story of Sheringham's fishing families and everything that affected them.

Henry 'Joyful' West, BEM, and Brian Pegg, BEM

Henry 'Joyful' West, BEM, Coxswain
Manchester Unity of Oddfellows
1963–1984

Brian Pegg, BEM, Coxswain
Manchester Unity of Oddfellows
1986–1989

Contents

Introduction

Fishing offshore is not just a job, and it probably never has been. Especially was this true of the time period in which this book is largely set, before the Norfolk fishing industry declined beyond recognition, as in so many other parts of our coasts. It was a tradition, a craft, a calling even, but above all it was a way of life, affecting whole families and whole communities. So it was in Sheringham.

Lower Sheringham, the fishermen's settlement, was very much the junior partner in earlier days, while Upper Sheringham – the richer and more ancient village – is mentioned in the Domesday Book, no less. Even when Lower Sheringham outgrew its inland neighbour, and was created an Urban District in 1904, it did not obtain full parish status until 1953, despite the fact that St Peter's Church had been built in 1897.

Early fishing forays from Upper Sheringham may have been towards the 'Old Hythe', between Sheringham and Weybourne. The settlement patttern in Lower Sheringham was dictated by the similarly lower cliffs and access to the shore, and the first cottages would probably have been built around Beach Road and the East Gangway, close to the stream flowing from the Common. The West Gangway area followed a little later. Fishing and its allied trades were prominent in both the West and East Gangway areas, around the cottages and in the narrow streets and yards close to the cliffs. There were whelk-coppers and smoke-houses; net chambers and rope-walks; tanning-coppers, chandlers shops, and boat-building yards. Close to the shore, Sheringham's fish auctions would take place, with the result decided by a gavel, in the form of two beach stones, being struck. Evidence is still there for those who look carefully, and many of the photographs that follow give an insight into this former lifestyle. Until the railway line brought new prosperity and recognition in 1887, Sheringham remained a fishing village, but even for many years after the town's southwards expansion, it was still, at its centre, dominated by the fishing industry.

Fishing communities such as Sheringham were, and are, closely knit, their families linked in mutual dependence upon this hardest of ways of earning a living. In early years fishing families were often desperately poor, and it was the sheer domestic genius of their womenfolk that saw them through the long days of winter. They looked forward to March, 'when the crabs crawl', because it was then that the hard times were over again, and money could be put back instead of just being spent. The living was uncertain and dangerous at the best of times, and at the worst of times families suffered the cruel loss of their loved ones, men in the prime of their lives.

Nevertheless, it was not a community without lightness and dry humour, or without merciless leg-pulling, where an error of behaviour or a particular quirk of character might result in a nickname lasting for more than one generation in a family. Nicknames are certainly a feature of Sheringham's local history. What kind of folk would visitors to Sheringham expect when they heard of Squeezer and Squinter, Belcher and Red Eye? Characters there certainly were, and the few token examples included in this book could have been multiplied again and again. To those families whose grandfathers and great-grandfathers equally deserved a place, had space allowed, we can only offer our apologies. These tough fishermen were also frequently deeply superstitious, and even their use of nicknames may have originated in the Middle Ages, when it was unwise to use a real name in case 'Old Nick' heard it. The same worry about 'familiar spirits' from the age of witchcraft may well have led to the fishermen's aversion to four-legged creatures. Even mentioning them anywhere near a boat was regarded as unlucky, especially rabbits for some unknown reason. Fishermen have been known not to go to sea that day if an animal crossed their path. And as for nuns and clergymen, any of the latter breed staying locally stood as great a chance of being taken out for a trip as swimming across the North Sea.

Today, the West Gangway is at the heart of what remains of this once-thriving industry, and the fascinating aerial photograph, shown below, allows us to see how things have changed.

The West Gangway, also known as the Fishermen's Slope, photographed before 1936 – the year the bridge was built across the Gangway.

The West Gangway, with the Two Lifeboats Inn and High Street can be seen top left; and the Flagstaff and Whelk-coppers bottom right, the latter cottage in its original form before restoration and enlargement in 1936. The coppers can be seen on the end of the cottage in the foreground, as can the accompanying chimneys. It was next to the Whelk-coppers that the early Lown boatyard stood, although the photo gives no clue to this. At the top of the Fishermen's slope, behind the two boats, is the *Henry Ramey Upcher* shed, as it is today. Alongside are the fishermen's sheds with the smaller shed to the right housing the old *Augusta* lifeboat. The former hand-winch can be seen at the top of the slope in the same position as the electric winch today.

Stand looking out to sea, somewhere along the North Norfolk coast, with little between you and the North Pole, perhaps when a winter gale is blowing spumes of salt spray in your face. And before you return to the welcome glow of the nearest pub, just imagine having to face such a sea in an open lifeboat, whose sole means of getting through those waves was muscle power. Remember also that before sitting down to row, these men had often run a mile along the cliff-top to the 'Old Hythe' with their heavy seaboots. Imagine straining with every sinew to get through those first dangerous yards of raging surf and, when sail was impossible, facing hours of similar physical effort, worth every second they would readily acknowledge, if a fellow seaman's life could be plucked from the edge. So lifeboat crews continue today in this spirit. It is a proud tradition. The fishing community of a town such as Sheringham and its lifeboat service are as interlocked as hand in glove.

Nor would it seem a coincidence that the spirit of service that underpins the RNLI is also supported in Sheringham's fishing history by a widespread religious faith, in the Salvation Army and Methodist traditions amongst others. Fishermen evangelists such as Willie Long, John 'Teapot' West and 'Tonny Dingy' Craske were born from these traditions. The Sheringham fishermen and their families, the 'Shannocks' as they have always been known, have a long pedigree. It is their story that this book tells, largely in their own words, and which, it is hoped, also pays tribute to them.

Alan Childs and Ashley Sampson

1. Early Beach Scene

Before the arrival of the railway in 1887, and the arrival of visitors in larger numbers, the main use of the beaches at Sheringham would have been connected with fishing. Boats would have been lined up the length of the beaches at the end of the day's work, and fishermen would be seen working close to their boats unloading the day's catch, repairing pots, preparing bait, mending nets or sails – generally busying themselves with the many tasks necessary to function effectively as fishermen.

A rare early beach scene on the East Beach, looking up from the lower beach towards cottages at the end of Beach Road

The West Beach, looking towards the Fishermen's Slope from the vicinity of the Two Lifeboats Hotel, before 1895 (the date the Upcher Groyne was built). The two rows of crab boats give a good indication of the steepness of the shingle beach; the boat at the low-watermark gives an idea of how far boats would have to be carried up the beach.

This busy scene at the foot of the Fishermen's Slope would have been typical on both East and West Beaches, with ropes, lines, buoys, whelk and crab pots seemingly scattered around. Further along the beach to the west, visitors would be using bathing tents.

Depending on the season, nets would be laid out to dry up to the 'Blue Steps' on the West Beach (west of the Fishermen's Slope and named after the blue brick used), and on the 'Tank' on the East Beach.

The balance between quite different and distinct uses of the beach was to change decisively during the twentieth century. At the beginning fishing was the predominant user, with the holiday trade getting a foothold. By the 1930s the balance might have been roughly equal. But by the 1960s fishing was in decline, and holiday-makers were the predominant beach-users.

Groynes

Groynes, or breakwaters, were built to try to stop the movement of shingle along the coast, thereby ensuring that the town had a good beach in front of it. For a long while, the Upcher Groyne on the West Beach was one of only a few groynes. More recently, the policy has been to build more groynes as part of the Council's sea-defence strategy.

---

2. Sixpennyworth of Bones

Fishing has always been a precarious living. The sea is an unreliable provider and families of fishermen often suffered genuine hardship. For the older people the fear of illness and the 'workhouse' were still very real. Between the years 1888 and 1909 the 'Two Lifeboats' coffee-house ran a 'Slate Club', providing a basic medical insurance for 6d. a week; the Friendly Societies such as the 'Oddfellows' and the 'Foresters' did the same. Most of the shops also ran Christmas Clubs to help families budget ahead. Nevertheless, one fisherman described the life as 'really primitive living' when compared with today:

We were really poor. My mother came home one night and she said: 'Father, poor Gladdy [her sister], *she hen't got one piece o' coal.' He opened the door of the coal-bunker that was underneath the stairs. 'Well you can take her a pailful of that and leave us a pailful.' That sort of life it was. We were contented somehow and we were happy; we were really happy, but poor.* (1)

The women frequently had the job of looking after the money:

Mother used to have this tin box, and when the visitors paid her it would go in the box. That was our box for the winter. If somebody's birthday was coming up, the money had to come out for the presents. That could only be touched in the winter months to get some money out if things were really bad. (2)

Despite these constraints, the womenfolk always seemed to provide good, nourishing meals for their families, as those who grew up in fishing families remember, almost without exception:

Food always seemed to be very wholesome and very good. Even if they were hard up my mother would always have butter. Mostly the men sat down to good stews and soups. Nearly always on the stove would be things boiling, like bones. They would go and get sixpennyworth of bones and put all their carrots and onions in it. You could also go down the bakeries and take a tray of things, and they would charge a penny for whatever item you left. (3)

Five generations: the old lady is Elizabeth 'Granny' Craske (née Cooper), 1806–1907. Just imagine, born the year after Trafalgar! She was 100 when the photograph was taken in 1906. Her daughter, Elizabeth Bishop, is seated, with *her* great-grandson Henry. Her son on the left is John Henry 'Christmas' Bishop, and the younger man is *his* son 'Jack Tar' Bishop.

Mr 'Dowsey' Little and his wife Ann (née West) inside the 'front room' of their house. Note the Victorian ornaments and the family Bible in a prominent position. 'Dowsey' Little was the original proprietor of the Grimsby Coal, Salt and Tanning Company, known to older fishermen as 'Dowsey's' (see p. 44).

In the cottages the 'front room' was often kept for special occasions, or if you were ill:
Mother used to say: 'Go down and put a little polish on for Granny West.' Her front room, the woodwork, table, sideboard and everything, just shone. She never left off doing her work. You hardly ever went in the front room unless you took visitors in, or if you were really ill. I remember I had whooping cough. There used to be a fire lit and that was wonderful to think we could go in and lay on the settee, and a great big fire. (2)

But the cloud hanging over all fishing families was the fear of tragedy at sea:
The dread of everyone's life really was hearing the mortars go off for the lifeboat. All of 'em who had anything to do with the fishing, half the population in Sheringham, would all rush home from school to see what was going on. (2)

The Slate Club

The membership number was unlimited (130 in the first year) between the ages of 16 and 45, and for your subscription you were entitled to '10/- a week for twelve weeks and 6/- per week for the next twenty weeks'. But be warned: 'If any Member shall, whilst in any foreign part, or in any town other than Sheringham or Beeston Regis, be afflicted with sickness, he shall not receive any benefit without a medical certificate.' And, of course, to receive benefits you would be 'on the club'.

---

3. Hailstones and Herring-bones

With the possible exception of Caister and Winterton, Sheringham was the only town in this area to have a gansey-knitting tradition. Ann West still knits for her husband Lenny; she uses five needles, although the number could vary from four to eleven according to the knitter's preference:

You have to have five fine needles and fine wool for Sheringham ganseys, and you knit it on the round, like you would a sock. Only the top half was patterned and just a small pattern on the sleeves. Patterns would be anything to do with fishing and the weather: lightning, hailstones, coil o' rope, mesh of the net [diamonds] open or closed – the one filled in represents the fish in the mesh, rope ladders, herring-bone – either up or down. Some families did have one special pattern, although they had other patterns as well. Or they would mix the pattern up. Say they liked 'meshes', they would then incorporate that in with other things. They are all 'set up' – they are all spaced out in boxes, evenly. The needles are usually about 14–16 steel needles,(occasionally seventeen) points each end so you can keep going round. The wool was just ordinary 3-ply blue wool. That was layed-up what we call tight; that wun't fluffy, and the pattern stood out nice; but you can no longer get that. My family used to send to Scotland to get the wool and that was right fine, what we call hard, not fluffy. Ganseys about here are the best you could get, because they're the finest. (4)

Olive Edis, working from her Sheringham studio and using natural light only, captured the character of the North Norfolk fishermen so vividly. The gansey pattern shown here is ladders, with coil o' rope.

These working ganseys being worn by 'Big John' Craske (left) and Ernie Grimes show the traditional division into patterned and unpatterned sections, and the patterning on the sleeves.

Knitting 'sheaths' or 'shields'
The older generation of knitters frequently used a sheath (in Norfolk called a shield) to help support the needle holding the work, thus taking the weight. Shields would often be stuck in their apron belts. Many older knitters could not manage without them. Some shields were leather pouches with straps, others were simply pieces of wood with a hole in the end for the needle. Some were finely finished and have become collectable.

In another family the grandmother is remembered as getting her pattern ideas in an unusual way:

She used to look at old photographs. She didn't have any pattern. She also used to go to Yarmouth because all the fisher-girls were always knitting. They used to make lovely ganseys. I think she just decided what she was going to do when she got there. She obviously knew exactly what every pattern was and how many stitches there were. She used to measure round people and then she would say: 'I think I'll put on five score and five.' They used to do the neck so tight I can remember my grandfather had a job to get it over his ears. She didn't have buttons. (5)

The fineness or otherwise of the gansey patterns would depend upon the skill of the knitter, the thickness of the wool and the size of the needles used. This delightful study, again by Olive Edis, shows Billy West wearing a gansey with a version of the lightning pattern.

15

4. He's Wearing his Sister's Hat

Fishermen's wives not only knitted ganseys but they often made most of the other items of clothing as well, as Hazel Cheney recalls:

My grandmother also used to make all my grandfather's underpants and vests, with the creamy hard stuff. They must have been ever so uncomfortable to wear. She used to put calico pieces on the top with lacings on them. And she even used to make his navy blue trousers with the flap. I suppose you couldn't get them anyhow else. All the slops she used to make. They used to wear them thick flannel shirts underneath their ganseys. (5)

Sunday best would obviously include their finest ganseys but in addition:

To smart up, round their neck they had a 'ropper' [wrapper], like a silk scarf, but lots of them were square, and they rolled them up and tucked them in their gansey. (2)

The thigh boots were originally of leather before rubber became available in about 1916 (forces' rejects it was suggested). A 'bootjack' was often used for removing them. The long boot stockings were made from a coarse greasy wool, called 'hob':

Mother used to say 'go round to Teddy Fiddy's and bring me some "hob", home,' and she would knit the stockings. They would also unwind it so that was one thread and they could knit vests with that. It was like two or three threads together, this 'hob'. (3)

Sealskin hats were commonly worn by the older generation of fishermen, often for Sunday best, or when having their photograph taken.

It may possibly be that Billy 'Cutty' Craske senior was the one responsible for bringing the peaked cap to Sheringham, which gradually replaced the sealskin hats and the 'chummies' of early photographs. He was in London, in the late 1890s, visiting the family of his bride to be and proudly wearing his sealskin hat:

When he was aware of a gang of cockney boys behind, who then taunted him with the chant: 'he's wearing his sister's hat'. A horrified Billy Cutty conformed: he bought a flat cap and, by bringing it back to Sheringham, he started the fashion there. (6)

And as for the fishermen's wives, one child of a fishing family remembers them as 'sober-looking, but they always looked nice. They always looked tidy, respectable':

You'd hardly see any older ones without a shawl on. The shawls [see p. 12] were knitted or crocheted mostly and they had tassels all the way round. Nearly everybody went about with them when the weather was cold. Long skirts were made of a sort of serge – gabardine and serge. And nearly everyone, when they were cooking, would wear an apron. (2)

Slops, oilskins and Bam-skins
A slop (see p. 22) was the practical outer
layer worn over the gansey. It was a
loose-fitting garment made of calico, and
tanned in the tanning copper. Oilskins
were made of thick, white, heavy-duty
calico, treated regularly with linseed oil
to make them weatherproof. Bam-skins
were made in the same way, and were
like a working apron.

A portrait, by Olive Edis, of Louisa West (née Little). Fishermen's wives of this generation wore darker colours, and the ubiquitous apron gave a hint of their lives. They might wear them anywhere, outside or indoors.

An Olive Edis portrait of 'Backs' Woodhouse in oilskin and sou'wester, but also wearing his 'ropper', probably for the photograph. It was quite common for the sou'wester to be worn indoors. When sun was more of a problem than rain or rough seas, the sou'wester could be turned round and thus provide a good sun-shield.

5. Everything by Eye

Lower Sheringham's boat-building history includes four family names: Boxall, Emery, Johnson and Lown. Sheringham supplied boats for Cromer, and for a good stretch of the North Norfolk coast. When Lewis 'Buffalo' Emery needed a new boat and as no one was able to oblige, he simply built one himself, thus starting the family firm. He went on to build the *Henry Ramey Upcher* lifeboat, (see p. 46) based on the crab-boat design. The third generation of the Emery family was represented by Reg, who died in 1957. A few years before his death he recorded his thoughts for a BBC programme called 'Down to the Sea' (1953).

My family has been building boats for the local fishermen for more than a hundred years and we're still doing so today. About 1870 my grandfather, Lewis Emery, had his four sons, James, Robert, Ben and John, working with him. And there were other builders at that time – Harry Lown and his nephew, Edward Skipper, and Robert and Tom Boxall. Between them they launched about twenty new boats every year.

Now the shape and construction of these boats hasn't altered at all in living memory, and there is no reason why they should, as they are perfectly suited for this part of the coast. They are double-ended, that is pointed at both stem and stern, and are quite open, having no deck of any sort. I have recently built them up to 30 feet for the whelk fishing at Wells and Brancaster, but the Cromer and Sheringham men want them about nineteen feet. They have a width of about seven feet and a depth of just over three feet, so they are quite beamy boats, and need to be for safety when handling pots in anything of a sea.

At Sheringham we are very proud of the fact that every boat is handmade, the only machinery we use being an electric drill. The keel, deadwood, stem and stern posts, which come out of best English oak, are cut with an ordinary handsaw and shaped with an adze. There are eleven planks on either side, made from oak and English larch, half an inch thick. Inside there are 36 timbers, or ribs, also of oak, which are steamed to shape, and fitted after the hull has been planked up. This is done clinker fashion [see p. 20]. We don't use any moulds at all. We do everything by eye and careful measurement. (7)

The Emery boat-shed was conveniently two-storeyed, but this did present problems. A large ramp and many hands were needed to move the completed boat from the upper storey.

This photograph is one of a set taken by H. H. Tansley capturing the atmosphere of the Emery workshop in about the 1930s. The lines of the boats in their earlier stages are reminiscent of the Viking craft which landed on Norfolk's shores, and are double-ended, as the Viking longboats were.

A remarkable photograph of the late 1930s showing three generations of the Emery boat-building family. It includes, from the left, Robert Emery, son of the founder; his son, Reg; Reg's sons Harold, and then Sid, as a boy – who did not go into the business; James, brother of Robert; and, finally, Reg's son, Chris. The boat is a whelker called the *Knot*, built for Gerald Bullard.

6. Boats, Bands and Pigeons

Bob Boxall had his boat-yard on Station Road in late Victorian times. He was also remembered as an organiser of the old town band and an expert bass player. Even earlier, Leonard Lown was building crab boats with his son Henry, first on West Cliff and then in Cremer Street. In 1898 they were joined by a keen young, 14-year-old apprentice. By 1906 this young man, Johnny Johnson, had taken over the business. He was a most respected builder, and by the time he retired at the end of 1949, he had built around 130 boats for North Norfolk and further afield.

His grandson remembers him in this way:

My grandfather, a builder of crab boats, was a very private person, who battled through the pain of ulcerated legs, which required dressing morning and evening, to earn a living, and satisfy the needs of the local fishing industry. He was very much a one-man band, except on days when timbers were steamed, to cope with the need to bend them to the shape of each boat, which was built by rule of thumb, no plans. His working day was spent standing or kneeling on the earth floor of a draughty boat-shed, or on the ribs of a boat, and this with ulcerated legs!

Away from work John was a devoted family man, who enjoyed a game of bowls in middle-age and who showed great patience when, as a pigeon-fancier, he waited to clock-in his racing birds. His young pigeons were often given their first flight home from Norwich when John, watching City play at 'The Nest', would attach a message to the leg of a bird showing the current score, before releasing it from a basket at half-time! (8)

Clinker Building

This is a term used in boat-building where the external planks are put on so that one edge of each overlaps the edge of the plank beneath it, like clapboards on a house. They would be fixed in place by copper nails and where the planks overlapped, the boat-builder would put hot tar in the joint to make it waterproof (caulking). If the planks butt each other, it is described as 'carvel' built.

Johnny Johnson (right) with old Bob Rushmer in front of the small shed in Cremer Street where 130 boats were built during his career.

John seldom left the county of Norfolk, and possibly his first steps outside the county were during the 1914–18 war when he was conscripted to work as a shipwright in Liverpool. Years after, I remember seeing a card which he had written in back-slang to his wife, greeting her from Liverpool.

Whenever a minor repair was needed to the Sheringham lifeboat John was called to patch things up. It would often be necessary for him to work all day at the lifeboat shed. During Hitler's war, May, his wife, was possibly the only woman in Sheringham to be given a pass to allow her on to the prom, to take him his dinner. Before that he was for some years either chief winchman or launcher of the lifeboat at the Old Hythe.

He was a God-fearing man, worshipping on Sunday evenings at the Methodist Chapel in Station Road, and frowning on anyone using bad language, particularly in his work-place. (8)

Boxall's boat-yard was at the top of Station Road. Fishermen could tell by eye the subtle differences in the boats from each builder. Boxall boats were said to be somewhat 'tubbier'.

A photograph taken when Sheringham seafront was made up just of pebbles, with not a boulder in sight! It shows the last generation of the motorised crab boats which have now virtually disappeared. From left to right the boats are *Englishman*, *Liberty* (hoveller), *Mizpah* (with Arthur Scotter), an unknown boat with Jimmy Allen, and *Miss Judith* (with Stanley Little).

7. 'Young Quilter'

The largest boat ever built in Sheringham was for Mr (later Sir) Raymond Quilter of Bawdsey Manor, Felixstowe. 'Young Quilter' enjoyed the company of Sheringham fishermen, dressed like them, and often lived amongst them. Aged about 20, he commissioned the 33-foot fishing smack, *The Three Sisters*, from Johnny Johnson, which was finished in 1924. Joe Pegg remembers the interest it aroused, not only in Sheringham:

While that was being built I can remember the fishermen coming from Cromer. Several of them older fishermen used to come and stand, having a chat with Johnny and looking at that boat. Them fishermen at Cromer were really interested in it. At the finish he couldn't close his doors. (9)

This was how the boat was described:
The beam is 12 foot and the depth four foot six inches. The general arrangements of this craft are workmanlike, fishing facilities having been the first consideration. A flush deck is provided forward, forming a 14-foot cabin, provided with a coal stove, a Primus cooking stove, seats and lockers. Two people at least can find comfortable sleeping accommodation. The engine is installed aft, being completely enclosed, whilst steering is by tiller. Amidships the craft has been left open, the floors having spaces between them and arranged below for a fish well. The power plant consists of a two-cylinder sleeve-valve Kelvin engine of 12–18 h.p. In addition to the engine, the sail power is considerable: a mainsail, foresail, jib and topsail are provided. The mast is 30 feet in height. (10)

Raymond Quilter seemed to pack into his brief 56 years of life what most would need six lives to achieve, as was indicated in one of his obituaries in 1959:
If a boy delights in lying on his back between the rails at night for the pleasure of watching express trains run over him, and can later claim to have been birched more times in a given period than any other Etonian, it may be taken as likely that he will grow up to be something of a 'character'. (11)

A Tansley portrait of Raymond Quilter of Bawdsey Manor, near Felixstowe. Notice the leather seaboots and the slop.

The 'principal serious work' of his life, for which he was rewarded by the Air Ministry, was the design of parachutes:

Now that he could no longer lie under trains, here was the perfect substitute. He made incessant descents, trying out new parachutes of his own design, often delaying their opening till his friends had given him up for lost. As a substitute for normal sport during the war, Quilter took up bomb disposal. Another of his 'lines' was designing diving suits, in which he naturally played the main experimental role himself. (11)

Raymond Quilter was often available in his diving capacity to sort out the Sheringham fishermen's problems, perhaps with fouled crab pots after a gale. But it was Quilter's connection with parachutes that very probably led to fishermen here being introduced to the new-fangled nylon cord for their pots:

First change was to parachute cord, after the war. There was a good market for that. If you knew where to go you'd get some cheap nylon. Billy Cutty used a lot of this, and that was good fishing stuff. Quilter of Felixstowe – that's how that started. That was a bit of a secret. Everybody wanted it! (12)

This photograph was used in an article featuring *The Three Sisters* in a magazine (then called) *The Motor Boat*. It took eight hours to get her to Felixstowe on her maiden voyage.

Raymond Quilter is in the centre and, to his right, his friend Teddy Fiddy. Notice the house in the background named 'The Mo', after Morag, the daughter of Sir Thomas Digby Pigott, a member of the Upcher family.

8. Pinkers and Hubblers

Today, there are comparatively few boats fishing from Sheringham, whereas in Victorian times there were, at the peak, over 200. Although the majority were the typical Sheringham 'crab boats', or later 'motor boats', there was still a variety of craft to be seen along the beach. There were pinkers and hovellers ('hubblers'), and 'Great Boats'.

A 'pinker' is a long, narrow boat and a hoveller ['hubbler'] *was a bigger boat than an ordinary crab boat, but on the same style, but that's wider than a pinker. A hoveller was a three-man boat. There was several here at one time. A pinker was right narrow. The pinker, they could get them off quick. We are talking years ago, in my grandfather's time. They used to use them for fishing, herring-catching and lining. The hoveller wasn't so big as the whelk boats. Whelk boats had what we call 'cuddies' or cabins built on so they could get out of the weather.*

What we call skiffs, the smaller boats, they had brass 'rollocks' for the oars that set into the top. Skiffs were only used more or less for people what had retired. Old 'Gofather' had a skiff. When they'd retired they'd go on their own, and have two or three crab pots. Or they'd take somebody for a trip. All the boat-builders used to make skiffs. (13)

Much larger boats were the so-called 'Great Boats'. Some were known as 'dandies' when they had a 'dandy rig'. They could be away for up to six weeks at times, fishing further north.

The 'Great Boat' was like a fishing smack. You couldn't beach 'em. You'd have an ordinary crab boat on board, and when the weather was fine, at weekends, you'd moor off here and then you'd row ashore in the crab boat. Monday morning you'd row back again. But if the weather was rough, you had to go either to Morston or to Blakeney where you could get in harbour with her, and tie her up there. Then walk home and walk back Monday morning to get aboard, which my grandfather used to do. There was no other means of getting there, less you knew somebody with a horse and cart. (13)

The 25-foot whelker *Marion* was built by Johnny Johnson for Mr Theobald Neilson, the Danish coxswain of the Wells lifeboat. Here it is being launched on 9th May 1930. These boats, with a greater range, were ideal for whelk fishing, which was carried on a great deal from Wells. Note the protective 'cuddy' or cabin which these larger boats, of necessity, contained.

Manhandling the boats through the streets of Sheringham was no easy matter, but the occasion usually drew a crowd of people, with many willing hands. The boat passing the 'Lobster' Inn is the whelk boat *William Edward,* built by the Emery workshop, and launched on 25th April 1949. The three men at the front are (from left to right) Joe Pegg, Jimmy 'Mace' Johnson and Old Bennett Middleton.

This boat is a hoveller ('hubbler'), a somewhat less common boat with at least a three-man crew, able to fish further out. There was still no cabin or protection.

This extremely rare photograph shows a variety of boat called a 'pinker'. The earliest of our rescue boats, *The Upcher* (see p. 46) was of this type. They were a more pointed boat, and could be launched more easily. They were sometimes used for salvage work.

9. Pots and Gear

This photograph shows an assortment of gear – the most prominent being the whelk pots against the boat, and some crab pots and ropes. Crab pots could also be used for catching lobsters, although for this purpose some fishermen made slightly larger pots with a wider 'crinny' or 'spout'. The fisherman here is holding a small barrel – an early form of wooden dan buoy, superceded by the more familiar, conical design about the beginning of the twentieth century.

The long hundred

The long hundred was a strange method of counting. It meant 120, but as crabs were counted in pairs, or 'casts' a long hundred of crabs was exactly 240, and fitted in with the money system then used (240 old pennies to the pound).

Fishermen made their own pots, as well as repairing them, and there could not have been many days when there was no work to do on them.

One little-appreciated fact is the part that blacksmiths had in the making of pots (as well as providing all the metal fittings for boats when they were built). The 'music' was the baseplate for the crab pot. Made of cast-iron, it provided the necessary weight for pots to stay on the sea-bed. The fisherman could then construct a wooden frame around the 'music' on which the wooden hoops and sticks were fitted – the framework for the pot.

The way the pot was braided was important – the net was braided on to the frame. But: *…this being rough, hard ground out here, when there come a breeze of wind the pots move about, and when they are hauled, the braiding would all be chafed off and gone. But, now we braid directly on to the sticks and bows as we go. At Cromer, they braid the net first and then lace the net on.*

Years ago, why pots took so much damage in a breeze of wind was because if you had a hazel, chestnut or elm bow, and you didn't change it when you repaired your pots, and well then they rotted through (at the bottom) and the first bit of weight came on they just cracked [see p. 59]. *That's why there were so many casualties. But now, with this here modern stuff* [plastic drain rods] *we don't encounter nothing like that.* (14)

Bob 'Rally' West working on a pot near the East-End slipway.

Once you get the spout in [the opening to let crabs into the pot], *a pot was like a house. Then, you braided in the four 'windows' either side of the spout. You then turned the pot up on its end, and you braided the gable end in, followed by the other gable end. Then you braided a piece along the top which was the 'roof', and left a space for the 'door'.*

When I used pot stuff, I could do a pot in an hour – but, not now! And, you can't braid this modern stuff as quick as you could that. Besides, that was something you was doing every day, because the manilla or sisal only lasted five to six weeks if you were lucky – it rotted away in the water. I used to sit on the prom sometimes, and do my braiding. (13)

The bottoms of whelk pots were also cast by the blacksmith (Jimmy High), and then eight irons were put in around and shaped – and they were actually wrought in there – and then they put a ring around the top, and that was sold as a skeleton to the fisherman.

The fisherman would then rope around, taking a turn around each post, all the way around and up to the ring at the top. Then, a strop was put on, and they'd put a little hanging net in, which stopped the whelks from coming out. Once they got in, they couldn't come up past that net. Inside, they have what we call a 'bar' – which is where a piece of fish was put – mostly herring – so that the whelks had to climb up the outside and drop in to get the bait. (15)

Old 'Billy Butcher' Johnson and Young 'Billy Butcher' Johnson. The pot being held by Old 'Billy Butcher' is only partly finished. The 'music' can be clearly seen, and some braiding is in place – the gable ends and two 'windows' – but, the spout, remaining 'windows' and roof have still to be added.

10. 'Orrock'-holes and Launching-off Poles

Sheringham's shingle beach has always presented daily problems when launching and recovering boats. If the top of the beach had steepened during a spring tide, it could be months before suitable conditions changed the slope. Lower down there might be a series of ridges produced by 'constructive' tides, making it extremely difficult to move boats in either direction. Before winches were introduced, boats were carried up the beach using their oars. As seen here, the oars were placed through the 'orrock'-holes, with ends resting on the thwarts, and the fishermen were then able to lift the boat and carry it up the beach.

The fishermen are, from left to right: John Craske, James 'Squinter' West, Christopher 'Cutty' Craske, William 'Billy Cutty' Craske, Christopher 'Stiffy' West, and William 'Billy Fiddy' West.

The crew of a two-man crab boat faced a problem in carrying their boat:
With two of you, you could only lift one end off the ground. As there used to be a lot of boats coming ashore at the same time, so two boats would join. There'd be four men, so you had your oars through four 'orrock'-holes, and that's the way you'd carry it down in the morning. (13)

Large boats wanting to get over the shingle and up the Fishermen's Slope were able to make use of large iron rings set in the concrete slope, or use the block-and-tackle method:
When boats came ashore to the edge of the stones and it was a heavy boat, they'd put a rope on it. Then take the rope to one of the rings, tie it around, and on the ring would be a pulley. The rope went through the pulley, and was taken right down the beach to where there were several fishermen, and they'd pull the boat up. (9)

Although crab-fishing was the main activity, boats also went after cod, herring, and mackerel, using nets or lines. A lantern in the boat would signal an all-night trip.

Some idea of how steep the shingle beach could be is seen in this launch. Several crews would work together as a gang. Each boat would be launched by the gang with just one man aboard. The last one or two boats off would also take the remaining crews of those boats already launched and transfer them once clear of the surf.

Another method of getting boats up the beach in suitable weather conditions was called 'knocking up'. This involved minimal effort, and relied on breaking waves to do the work. The boat was left broadside on at the watermark, and water from the breaking wave would gradually nudge or 'knock' the boat up the beach.

A launching-off pole, or quant, was used for lifeboats [see p. 47] as well as crab boats when conditions were difficult, to ensure greater control at the critical moments after the boat entered the water, and before it was under way, using oars or an engine.

The *Britisher* being launched from the East Beach with a quant.

11. Skeets and Winches

When not being carried, boats were either pushed or pulled across the shingle, and skeets made this task much easier, as well as ensuring less damage to the hull of the boat. This preference for skeets – wooden blocks containing two wheels over which the boats keel would run – came in with motor boats, which were too heavy to lift and carry. The use of skeets has remained a feature of boat movement throughout the period of the traditional Sheringham-built wooden, motorised crab boats.

Each boat had two skeets, and you would grease them up at night because that was the easier and only way of getting down – we didn't have carriages then. You could always tell when someone hadn't greased the skeets, especially on the sand; you'd run along lovely and, all of a sudden, you'd get CRRRR ... and then the language come out! (12)

Following the use of ropes, and block and tackle to pull boats up the beach, hand-winches were introduced:
There were two down on the East Beach – one half-way to the 'Tank' from the slip, and another on the slipway. There were hand-winches on the Fishermen's Slope, on the 'Blue Steps' and on the Admiralty Slip. Hand-winching was more than a three- or four-man job, and that was nearly as hard work as hauling pots. They used to shout out 'put 'em in Long, Tom', and you'd stop heaving, and put them in a different gear when the weight came on. (1)

This group of fishermen, including Harry Dyball on the right, are using the hand-winch situated on the Admiralty Slip. Note the cable going off to the left. Electric winches were introduced in 1936, after this photograph was taken.

Getting the boat down the beach could be difficult:

A hook spliced on one end of a four-inch rope was attached to a ringle fixed on the Prom. Long enough to go to the water's edge, the rope was taken to the first boat where, using a strong pole with a strong iron hook on the bottom, it was hooked in the propeller opening. The rope was then put with one turn at the bottom of the pole, and the top of the pole was then made fast to the bits near the stern-post with a good rope. It was then ready to lower the boat down the beach, keeping the rope at the bottom of the pole. One man worked the rope, other crew-members worked the skeets and held the boat upright. (1)

Billy Grice (left) is removing a skeet, and 'Demon' Cooper is holding the rope, while the boat is being held level by Jimmy Allen and 'Butterballs' Grice (right). Note that the boat is on two skeets to prevent it laying fast. The lowering-down pole, as it was known, can be seen behind 'Demon' Cooper's right shoulder: the rope went round this pole rather than the stern-post, since day-in and day-out use would have worn out the stern-post.

First hand-winches, and then electric winches, were to make the recovery of boats so much easier across the steeper shingle beach. The wire only extended to the edge of the shingle, and boats still had to use skeets across the sand. At first glance, both boats look as though they are being winched up the beach. However, while both are using skeets, one is attached to a rope, and the other to a winch-cable – the steep shingle beach makes lowering a boat just as difficult. Electric winches were bought by Sir Edward Meyerstein and located on the East Beach and the West Gangway.

The *Joan Elizabeth* being winched up the beach. Already on one skeet, the boat is held upright, while being guided on to the next one (in the foreground).

12. Shanks and Buoy-tows

The method of working the crab pots has changed over the years.

I can remember when they didn't work with shanks of pots. Because they were rowing and sailing, then they used 'swummers' in a line – single pots in a line – and my grandfather used to haul these 'swummers'. In a rough sea, they'd wash ashore and tangle. They'd row down the tide if you were going west'ard close inshore and then go out and haul the 'swummers'.

On the fishing side, round hoops were used, with lead at the top, and a long net. You put some bait in, chuck 'em out, and all of a sudden, pull 'em up. They had rows of hoops like rows of 'swummers', and you had to snatch them and keep a-coming – to keep the bag in, you see. You'd get nice dabs and lobster. (1)

'Corporal' Grice throwing a pot over the side.

Through most of the twentieth century wooden crab pots were used, gradually giving way to larger metal-framed pots called parlour pots.

We used to work them in 20s, 22s or 25s – which is called a 'shank'. Now, to make a shank up, you had a buoy on one end, with a flag on. Down from that buoy ran a tow, which was a buoy-tow, which went down to a strop on an anchor, which was a piece of rope with two eyes spliced in, and that was tied on. Then, a length of rope from the next eye on the anchor went to your first pot. Then, from that pot, ran another tow, and there was either 20, 22 or 25, and, of course, on the other end, you had an anchor, a buoy-tow, and a buoy. Each tow was 14 to 15 fathom apart.

You had to pull the pots off the bottom by hand. You'd steam along to them and pick your tow up, pull your buoy-tow in. You'd put the buoy for'ard, pull the buoy-tow in, which went down aft, then the anchor would come, and you'd put that for'ard, then the next pot would come. You'd bait that up and put that in what we called the fore-room, and the tow would go down aft. You'd haul them all like that, and they'd be stacked up in the fore-room.

Then, you'd go wherever you wanted to, and throw the buoy over and let the buoy-tow run out and throw the anchor over, let the tow go, and then hurl your pot over. Then, the next one, then shoot the pot away again, till that lot was done, and you'd go and do it again. So, you had all your pots from one shank in the boat at one go. You had to stack them and know how you stacked them. (13)

When they went to sea, the pot was made fast with a line to an anchor at one end with a rope up to a buoy, and the other end of the rope went to another pot. There were about 24 to 25 pots, all in a shank, and there'd be another anchor and another buoy. They'd pick the buoy up, haul in the first pot, empty that out, with the whelks put into nets called 'washers'. That's how they were brought ashore – carried across the beach on the back up the 'Blue Steps' to the old whelk-coppers, where they'd be boiled. That was such hard work – they might row twenty miles there and back, and, when they came ashore, they would have to carry the washers of whelks up to the coppers. (15)

Whatever the catch, baiting up was a daily task, and mostly done on the beach. In this scene, the shells on the stones suggest that the fisherman is breaking whelks up, and he is baiting the pack of lines to his left.

In this early photograph at the East End, the fisherman in the boat seems to be making some adjustment to the distinctive whelk pot. The strop can be seen, with a corked line resting on an oar.

There were six to eight whelk boats on the West End. Mostly, there were three fishermen in each whelk boat, and they'd go out to the whelk grounds – just yon side between Blakeney and Wells – somewhere between ten to twelve miles to sea.

Harry Johnson owned the whelk coppers [see p. 38], and he used to come out especially if there was a gale of wind coming – he'd look across to the Coastguard Station, look at the mast to see if a cone was up. He'd be concerned about his whelk boats, because he owned the boats, and let them off to the fishermen in those days.

He'd be concerned about the weather, because those boats had to come perhaps twelve miles back to Sheringham, and to land on the stony shore here was awkward in a rough sea. (9)

13. Nicking Crabs

Crabs and lobsters were sent away by train – alive. Because they were likely to bite or crush each other, and arrive 'damaged', steps had to be taken to overcome this. Crabs had their claws 'nicked' – cutting a muscle which prevented the claws from working.

The photograph on the front cover shows a slight variation on this theme, and is more to do with supply and demand: Bob 'Rally' West and Teddy 'Fiddy' West are nicking the crabs and putting them into the pot (also called a 'mooring box') to go and moor them off. They'd fill the pot up with the nicked crabs, and put them out to sea till the next day. *'Downtide', or whoever was buying the crabs would say they didn't want any that day, because they hadn't sold yesterday's.* (15)

String is being used to tie the claws of the lobster on the left, while another lobster is about to be tied up and the 'snewd' is ready on the thwart.

But, with a lobster, the claws could not be nicked, so the fishermen used string or 'snewd' to tie their claws:

In the finish, some bright spark got an old bicycle inner tube, cut little bits off and made them into elastic bands. They just put them over the claws, two twists and it was tight, and that did it. (15)

They used to go up to Mundesley, and they'd do two hauls, sometimes three a day. I know when they was off Overstrand way, they came ashore one day with three hundredweight of lobsters. They knew all the spots. They wouldn't tell you!
(1 and 12)

Old Billy 'Cutty' Craske in the centre with a catch of crabs and lobsters. He, and his sons, Young Billy 'Cutty' and Teddy 'Lux', were good at catching lobsters.

Any opportunity was taken to try and find where, in relation to the shore, these secret spots were. Brian Pegg describes one occasion when he tried to discover the famous 'King John' lobster location, known only to the 'Cutty' Craske family. The lifeboat had been launched while Teddy 'Lux' Craske (the mechanic) was out fishing, and Brian saw an opportunity.

Teddy was at sea, hauling on 'King John'. I said to 'Downtide', 'put me on board the 'Billy Cutty' ('cause Teddy had a good record – he never missed a boat, and that was going to blot his record), when we get alongside, I'll jump in, and Teddy can come aboard'. Teddy said 'no, no you're doing a good job' and Billy 'Cutty' said 'you lot can manage can't you?' I said we could, no problem, but, they'd rather have Teddy. I thought I could learn where 'King John' was.

As soon as I started, Billy 'Cutty' called 'look at that pot, that nearly went off'. And every time I looked ashore, he distracted me. So, when he was hauling away, I was looking, I thought 'there's the mill, there's the … Landmarks had to be lined up as 'meets'. 'Look what you're doing,' he'd say, 'don't look about.' He didn't give me four minutes to look, and when we got ashore, the lifeboat crew all asked me, 'Where's "King John"?' I said he wouldn't let me look! (12)

While Sheringham may be best known for its crabs and lobsters, other catches were important at different times and in different seasons:

Whelking was very important here in the winter-time. You either went whelking or you went long-lining for cod. You couldn't do the two, because you had to row right down to near Blakeney to your pots and row back again. (13)

Mackerel 'railing' required a very different approach to pots or nets. It needed: *A length of line or 'snewd' with a lead on the end – which you made yourself with a piece of thick wire across the centre. That wire, with eyes at both ends, was sealed in the molten lead. Another piece of snewd was attached to the eye, and then you'd have a spinner – a piece of shiny metal bent in different directions – to which was attached a hook with three hooks. On the end of that was another ring, and that piece of brass went right down the centre of the spinner, and that also spun and glittered in the water.* (13)

Carrying ashore the first catch of the season – a ped full of crabs – some of the 300 they caught that day. Fisheries Officer, Kitchener Pegg is talking to Arthur Scotter and 'Hof' Creasey (all are also carrying lobsters in their hands).

14. Forty More the Shilling

Sheringham in days past was a town dominated by the fishing industry, with numerous sub-trades and outlets for marketing the catch. And in one sense fishermen were ruled by the fishmonger, who might not want their catch that day. In earlier times the marketing might be from a cart, as with Thomas Isaac Craske, and 'Bloomin' Pegg, both of whom had local fish rounds. Hannah Piggott had a shop in Wyndham Street but also used a lorry for her village fish round, as 'Jodrell' Dennis remembers:

I have been out with Hannah Piggott. We've been all round Salthouse, Cley, Wiveton. 'Forty more the shilling, longshore herring, forty more the shilling.' I can see her now, that great old bell clanging and we had this ton lorry and that was full o' longshore herring. And she used to scoop 'em – never weighed 'em, of course – and I can still see these dear little old ladies out of the country, coming up. (16)

Henry 'Downtide' West's fish business became one of the biggest. He had first gone to sea aged 13 with his father, and his uncle, Bob 'Bumshee' West. 'Downtide' was later to be Coxswain of both the *Forester's Centenary* and the *Manchester Unity of Oddfellows*, the latter boat presented when Henry West was Director of the Order of Oddfellows.

West's shop at the bottom of the High Street. In later years a furore broke out when the local planning office wanted to move the decorative sign around the shop (not shown here). A public petition was mounted and succeeded in gaining a reprieve. Henry West is on the right and Henry Dale on the left.

In 1922, just before Henry West married, he bought a shop in Co-op Street, to turn it into a fish shop. Then in the late 1920s he moved to the shop in the High Street and then from there he began the wholesale business of sending the crabs and lobsters to people all over England, and also he used to boil whelks as well. In those days there were tons of crabs caught, long hundreds [see p. 26]. One boat would catch about four or five long hundred. After the war he opened a crab factory and did the potted crab and lobster, and bloater. We did the only 100 per cent pure crab in all England.
(17)

Aunt Dolly was almost an institution in 'Downtide's shop. She had come there aged 15 to help out for a bit, and stayed until she was 80. She must have dressed thousands of crabs.

Down the High Street a little was a smaller fish shop called 'Joyful's:

Grandfather 'Joyful' had to give up the sea so he opened a small shop at the top of Gun Street, where he lived, with Grandmother selling the crabs in the shop. Grandfather soon had a crab round. We boiled the crabs at Myrtle House. When Grandfather retired, my father Bob 'Joyful' and mother ran the shop, and I boiled for them. Father also had a crab round, same as Grandfather's. I took crabs on a trade bike instead of a barrow – two or three hotels with dressed crabs. My brother Jack took on the crab shop after father finished, keeping it in the 'Joyful' family. (1)

'Downtide' West and George Mann boiling crabs. This was a coal-fired copper, but gas-fired coppers were later used for the Crab Factory.

As with many other retailers, 'Joyful's early business included a delivery round in the local area. Customers expected to be able to buy fish, plus many other commodities, all absolutely fresh from the barrows and carts.

'Downtide' and 'Joyful'

Henry 'Downtide' West was at sea, rowing their boat, when his father ran a fish hook into his finger. Asked later how it happened, Henry replied that it had been caused by his rowing downtide at the time. The name stuck. Henry 'Joyful' West's great-grandfather was the first to be given the nickname 'Joyful', from his habit of singing hymns such as 'Joyful Canaan'.

15. Just a Red Herring

The main whelk-coppers in Sheringham for many years were run by the local businessman Harry Johnson, whose ventures were closely linked to the fishing community. Boats were rented by Johnson, who then bought their catch. He also made it possible for some of the first engines to be fitted:

There was an office there as well, a building next to where they boiled the whelks. He used to have two men boiling the whelks, one was Russell Johnson and the other was 'Brigham' Bishop, and Joe Farrow at the finish. The coppers were about four feet in diameter and at the back there would be one big oak post let into the brickwork with more like a crane that would swing, with a cable on to grip the big steel drum with holes all in it that had the whelks in. They would go down into the hot water, boiling 'em. And as they pulled them up again you'd see the water all drain back into the copper. Then they'd swing it round, drop it to the ground and they'd tip the whelks all out and they'd shovel them into sacks. They had a dray with a pony and they'd take perhaps 40 or 50 bags o' whelks up to the railway station. (9)

Sheringham is said to have had at least five whelk-coppers running at the beginning of the last century. This one, situated at the top of 'The Driftway', was owned by the Craske brothers. In this photograph of about 1900, we see Old Bob Craske (left), and his son 'Tonny Dingy' (centre). The fisherman on the right is unknown.

In this earlier period almost all fish shops had smoke-houses and coppers. Smoking herring added a particular flavour to the fish, but it was also a means of preserving them in the days before refrigeration.

You sold the fish what we call white, and most fish shops had smoke-houses. That was a building where there was racks across all the way up and an opening at the top to let the smoke out. You lit the fire under all these after you speted 'em, and burnt oak, which didn't flare but that kept red and smouldered. Bloaters and red herrings was a poor man's meal one time. (13)

Before herring were smoked, they were speted, that is, pierced through on a long stick or spete, usually about sixteen herring to a spete, with a finger width between. The spetes would then be arranged on the racks around the smoke-house. Here doing this job we see 'Tonny' Craske again, in a much later photograph.

Another of the fresh fish shops in Sheringham High Street was run by Robert Henry 'King Kong' Grice. Documents relating to the shop include an interesting letter of September 1916 from a Grimsby wholesale fish merchant, commenting upon the war: 'we are getting our full share of Zepps now here and the subs have sunk nineteen more of our trawlers – fish will be more scarce'.

Red Herrings

Red Herring were too strong for some people's taste. This is not surprising as they were smoked for at least a fortnight and then salted for two days! The frequently used saying referred originally to dragging this strongly flavoured red herring across a fox's path and so misleading the hounds.

16. Sail- and Rope-making

Sail-mending outside sheds near West Cliff, with Tom 'Barnes' Cooper looking on.

All early crab boats were rowing and sailing boats, with the lugsail the only form of sail used. Sail-making was, therefore, a feature of the fishing community, and was another of the fisherman's skills – or, at least, sail repair. Sail-making was not listed as an occupation in the nineteenth-century census returns for Sheringham – unlike rope-making, net-making or twine-spinning – and the skill was lost quite quickly as all boats went over to engines.

Essential requirements for all fishermen were rope and twine – both in the construction of nets and pots, and in their subsequent use. Made of sisal or manilla, the early ropes – even when tanned or tarred – did not last indefinitely, unlike modern nylon. The nets of crab pots, which were continuously submerged, rotted in a matter of weeks, and were regularly renewed.

Rope- and twine-making were, therefore, important jobs in a fishing community. Other than knowing there were rope-makers and twine-spinners, little evidence remains in Sheringham. There is no photographic evidence of rope grounds (or rope-walks), although they are thought to have been located in High Street, Holway Road (the forerunner of Station Road) and Cromer Road, and census returns showed rope-makers lived in these areas.

Rope-walks were where they spun the rope – which was usually a long, narrow piece of ground, because on account of them running the rope out and the twine out to spin it, to lay it up. There was one rope-walk just over my back wall, and that was nothing only a long rough piece of ground with his old shed down the bottom, where he used to spin it. The rope was either laid up hard or soft – that's the turn in the rope – you either got a piece of rope what's right hard and you can hardly open it, or you get a piece of soft rope. That'd either be laid [or twisted] left-hand or right-hand which, on a herring net, you had to have one of each.

A walk would have posts at one end, and he'd have an old shed. My father, when he was young, with the old fella being over the back, Saturdays they used to go and help him to spin the rope and the tows, and when he'd done, he'd give them a ball of pot-stuff for his father to braid the pots with. (13)

A crab boat lowering its lugsail
as it approaches the shore.

The ropes had to be treated with 'ponica' or 'kutch' to give the sisal or manilla strength and to make them last longer. *You bought it from Uncle Teddy in Beeston Road shop, and that came in great big hardwood boxes. He'd say, 'What you want – "Ponica"?' So, he'd take a chisel and knock off a lump of 'ponica' – like toffee, but much harder. You took home whatever you wanted to make the tan. That was the first preservation you put in the rope. Now, how you done that, you melted it down, the stronger the better, and they used to put them* [the ropes] *in tubs and let them soak in there weeks. And when you got them out, they were a lovely brown colour, and that had gone through into the rope.* (13)

41

17. Net-making and -mending

Net-making and -mending were exclusively womens' jobs, and the 1851 census identifies fourteen girls in fishing families as net-makers. Fishermens' wives, while not listed, would certainly have continued their net work. It is interesting to note that the 1851 census identifies far more net-makers than other census returns, and it may be that the enumerator was being far more diligent than others, or that instructions or categories were different for that census.

This 1897 photograph shows what must have been a typical beach scene, with nets spread out to dry behind the woman. The fisherman is looking on, while she mends the net, making it ready for the next trip.

Jimmy 'Mace' Johnson, watching his wife Augusta mend a net in the yard of 'Bon Accord' in Victoria Street.

Lenny 'Teapot' West is the last fisherman who has also been a net-maker and -mender:

Fishermen, years ago, could mend a net provided it wasn't too bad, but they couldn't set them up – unless they were trained to set them up. My father learnt that from his grandmother. When she was a girl, that was her trade. So, she passed that on – she never had no girls, so, she passed it on to my father. And, of course, he passed that on to me, and then I used to get the job of doing everybody's nets.

You wouldn't braid a whole net now. But, sheets of lint [manufactured net] can be bought, and a net set up. This is putting the corks on, the ropes on, and the norsels on [which link the top of the net to the rope above].

Some people, if they braid a net, they have a gauge – a piece of wood the size of the net they want – and they go round the wood and form the knot, and then pull the piece of wood out, and do the next row, and they will all be the same size. But, by use, you can do it with your eye and fingers. When there's a hole, you have to make the mesh the same size, otherwise you get a pocket.

Nylon nets are used now, because cotton nets are out. With a [very light] net like that in the photograph, it doesn't soak up water. That's why I have to put a leaded line on the bottom, so that hang down.

But, with a cotton net, when you put it in the water, we used to throw water over it first, and the cotton would soak the water up. With its extra weight, the net would hang down straight. (13)

Lenny West mending a net with needle in one hand and penknife in the other. The needles were handmade from wood, or even bone left over from the Sunday joint.

18. The Great Grimsby Coal, Salt & Tanning Co. Ltd.

No longer a shop, the building that housed the only chandlery between Yarmouth and Blakeney, can still be seen on Beeston Road. It stands empty, and doesn't give a hint of its former importance to the fishing community of Sheringham and a considerable stretch of the North Norfolk coast.

The Great Grimsby Coal, Salt & Tanning Co. shop on 9th August 1912. 'Dowsey' Little – the manager – is standing against a typical chandlery window display (including the tide times for the day).

The Great Grimsby Coal, Salt & Tanning Company had several branches along the east coast. In Sheringham its branch was run by Teddy 'Fiddy' West, who was also a fisherman. When he was at sea, his wife would run it. But, mostly, that was left to him – he ran the shop all his working life. Fishermen used to come from Cromer to buy pot stuff for their pots – there wasn't a chandlery in Cromer. (9)

Teddy 'Fiddy' had the shop when I was a kid. My grandfather used to call it 'Dowsey's', because the bloke who had it before him was called 'Dowsey' Little. When they [the fishermen] wanted pot-stuff – either manilla or sisal – it was in the winter. They weren't getting any income from fishing – so, he used to put it on 'tick' till they started crabbing. When they started, they'd pay. (15)

You went up the steps into that doorway and the lovely smell of the rope that met you, and up on the shelves would be different coils of rope, lanterns – all sorts of things for the ships and boats.

People would come miles to Teddy's shop. There would sit Teddy braiding a crab pot and my Aunt Myrtle would come in from the house and she would serve people. You could buy things by the yard, you could buy a net needle, the pot stuff, and all sorts of things.

That was a lovely little shop. An old barometer hanging in the window so you could see the weather. And there would be sou'westers and slops they'd sell. All those sort of things would be hanging up.(3)

While there was no other chandlery, fishermen could still choose where to buy their supplies.
The Gourock Rope Company used to come round, and they'd sell you rope a lot cheaper than 'Fiddy' could. The same old story: this shop used to belong to the Great Grimsby Coal, Salt & Tanning Co., and they used to put supplies in there.

Teddy 'Fiddy' West

'Fiddy' was the manager, and he sold them. This bloke from Scotland used to come down; he supplied my grandfather, although grandfather also used to go to the Grimsby shop and buy the pot-stuff occasionally, or this ponica, or, perhaps, hooks. When they were baiting line, they wanted 200 hooks on a pack of lines – so, you wanted 500 to 600 hooks at a time. And, of course, Grimsby Coal, Salt & Tanning Company still sold them stuff, because they used to pay. (15)

Ships' Chandlery
A shop specialising in all kinds of goods required by the owners of vessels, large or small. This was often the raw materials to make crab pots, nets, clothing – whereas, today, most of these goods are bought ready-made.

---

19. For the Use of the Parish

The Upcher family of Sheringham Hall were benefactors to the Sheringham fishing community. They provided the first 'rescue' boat, the *Upcher*, and subsequently two private lifeboats. The first was the fondly remembered *Augusta* and the second the *Henry Ramey Upcher*. They gave the town the 'Two Lifeboats Coffee House', a temperance establishment with a reading-room, and also provided soup-kitchens. There would be gifts of coal at Christmas and a charity was set up called the Ploughlet, designed to help Sheringham people. Even as early as 1826, Charlotte Upcher was showing her concern:

> Monday July 17th
> Spent the evening at Lower Sheringham. Harry West cast down. His baker's bill amounting to 9/-, he had only earned 4/- since March. Desiring to improve his condition I offered to lend him money to build a boat on a larger scale than those in use. He was much pleased; looks upon it as an answer to prayer. (18)

This boat, the *Upcher*, was the forerunner of the lifeboats. It even rescued a cat and a canary! Charlotte Upcher then arranged for the *Augusta* to be built. Launched in 1838, it remained in service for 56 years. It is usually credited to Robert Sunman, but may have been built by 'Old Newlyn' (probably William Lown).

Many familiar faces can be seen in this Olive Edis photograph. It is worth five minutes with a magnifying glass. Can you spot: Jimmy Dumble, 'Coaly' Cooper, Abraham Cooper, Tom 'Gayton' Cooper, 'Go-father' Pegg, 'Lody' West and Jimmy 'Paris' West?

When the question of the crew's payment was mooted, the new coxswain, Robert Long, who had taught himself to read and write, penned this fine letter to Charlotte Upcher.

I think it will be best to have this boat stand for the use of the parish and to have no fixed crew, but that whoever is at home, and will volunteer, and embark on any useful expedition, the boat to be at their service. I thought to offer them money, and to say, 'if you will go to sea to save these men, I will give you so much money', I return to say there are few men in this parish that dare venture to go to sea with such a view. I therefore suggest that they go to sea with the disinterested motive of doing good and that in the name of the Lord, who I trust will take charge of this boat. This I am sure is the ground we like to stand on. Not indeed that our people are not very needy, but we have never found our kind-hearted and benevolent friends behindhand in rewarding every benevolent and industrious enterprise.
I am Madam, your servant,
R. Long.

The second 'Upcher' boat was provided in 1894 by Mrs Caroline Upcher in memory of her husband. It also had a fine record of service, finishing in 1935. Its last trip was on VJ Day 1946, with a boatload of sightseers and very few fishermen to row. It was a sad and rather ignominious finale, as Bill Thirtle remembers:

I was sitting quite close to the mast when we sailed out; when we come about they didn't shift her tack so we come in what we call 'back-sail'. The sail rested on the mast and that spewed the wind out both sides. We lost a lot of way. We went more or less straight out but then as we tried to come straight in we finished up off Beeston Hill. Jimmy 'Coaly' Cooper waved his handkerchief and they fired the gun, and the 'Forester's Centenary' come and towed us in. When we come in that was quite rough on the beach. (15)

One of the last trips of the *Henry Ramey* under full sail. The photograph shows the 'quant' or 'launching-off', pole' being used, necessary to give the boat a helping hand in a heavy sea.

20. The *J C Madge* (1904–1936)

One of 35 lifeboats on the National Register of Historic Vessels considered to be of historical importance. As a rowing and sailing lifeboat, she differed from others in her class by being 41 feet in length and having an extra set of oars – eight instead of seven. This was at the request of the Sheringham lifeboatmen.

Being a rowing boat, it was vital that the crew could bring as much strength to bear on the oars. They needed something on the deck to push their feet against. 'Foot spoons' were built into the deck for this purpose. These were also found in the old crab boats and, if necessary, an old oar could be broken to make the 'foot spoon'.

As the RNLI lifeboat, the *J C Madge* served alongside the private lifeboat, the *Henry Ramey Upcher*, which had been in service since 1894 and was withdrawn from service in 1935. These were Sheringham's last rowing and sailing lifeboats.

The 'J C Madge' was one of the best sailing lifeboats there was if you'd hang in her! Soon as she shoved off the beach there's two tanks, one for'ard and one aft – the bungs filled full, stabilised her. And, as soon as we got to the anchor to get the mast and sail up, the first thing we did was pull a great iron centreboard down into the sea – she'd never turned over. But, the job was keeping in her! We all had a bit of rope about one foot and a half long with a big cork on. When that come a big 'un [wave], we bent our heads down and hung on to this rope until it was gone. (20)

There was no cabin in which to shelter and, once at sea, there was virtually no communication with the land, other than semaphore.

The longest, and most famous, rescue the *Madge* was involved in, took a total of four days from launch to return. In 1916, she put to sea to help the *SS Ulla* in the dark, with a snowstorm setting in [see p. 60].

This rescue took her to the Humber Estuary with the *Ulla*, where the crew were fed by Grimsby families – many of whom had Sheringham and Salvation Army connections. No communication with Sheringham was possible, though, because the land-lines were down.

The crew's families knew nothing of the fate of the *Madge* until its return four days later.

The *J C Madge* outside the Old Hythe lifeboat station.

Photo courtesy of Eastern Counties Newspapers

On its withdrawal from service, the *J C Madge* was sold into private ownership, and spent many years as a pleasure craft. It underwent considerable modification, with a large cabin constructed. The masts and rigging were also altered, and the 'Madge' became more of a sailing cruiser.

Seen here, off Brancaster in March 1989, this was to be her final journey under sail, before being transformed into a lifeboat once again (see p. 76).

21. The *Foresters Centenary* (1936–1961)

This was Sheringham's first motor lifeboat, but she still had masts and sails in case the engine failed. A new lifeboat house was built nearer the town just after the *Foresters Centenary* arrived on station, at the end of the West Beach promenade. This significantly shortened the distance crewmen had to run to the lifeboat and improved response times.

During the Second World War, the *Foresters Centenary* became known as the 'Airmen's Lifeboat', because of the number of times it rescued ditched aircrews returning to their Norfolk airfields from raids on Germany. In fact, many nights were spent at sea for this express purpose.

Taken in 1936, shortly after the *Foresters Centenary* arrived on station and moved into its new lifeboat house. Manpower was still needed to pull the lifeboat for launching. During World War II this task was often done by soldiers billeted in the town, as many fishermen were away in the forces.

New Lifeboat House

Nearer the town than the previous lifeboat house, it was on a very restricted site at the foot of the cliffs, which meant that the lifeboat house could not face the beach. A turntable and a long slipway had to be constructed to improve launch times.

The *Zor* rescue is one of the memorable post-war rescues undertaken by the *Foresters Centenary*.

Wells lifeboat had already taken some of the crew off, when we got the 'shout', as the 'Zor' had developed a heavy list; her position was 22 miles NNE of our station. When we arrived on the scene, the 'Zor's timber had started to float overboard.

'Downtide' West put the lifeboat amongst the timber where the crew were, but they wouldn't come, as it was too high. At this time, a halyard snapped and more timber went overboard.

We went round to the port side that was high out of the water. The 'Zor's crew lowered a ladder and ropes, while the coxswain held the lifeboat alongside. The remaining crew of five came down the ropes, helped by the lifeboat crew. All this time, a tug had a tow-rope made fast on the 'Zor', and as soon as the crew were off, the tug took the strain. It was the last of the 'Zor': she went down stern first.

We returned to our station leaving tons of timber floating where she had gone down, arriving back at the beach two and a half hours later. (1)

Recovering the *Foresters Centenary* across the beach, with boards keeping the keel off the sand. Among those keeping the lifeboat upright are Lenny 'Teapot' West and Brian Pegg.

Out of the water, its lines can be clearly seen, earning it the affectionate nickname of 'the peapod' – then and now.

The *Foresters Centenary* returning with some of the crew of the *Zor*.

22. The *Manchester Unity of Oddfellows* (1961–1990)

Picture by the Eastern Daily Press, Norwich

This launch off the carriage shows the use of a feature unique to the
Sheringham lifeboat. The quick-release pin is about to be pulled.

The *Manchester Unity of Oddfellows* was a 37-foot Oakley-class boat with twin diesel engines. With 29 years continuous service, she was the longest-serving lifeboat of this class. The Sheringham lifeboat had a unique feature – a quick-release mechanism that was said to be an unnerving experience for any visiting coxswain unfamiliar with it.

The quick-release mechanism never let us down – it was absolutely brilliant. It was the shortness of the beach and the steepness of the ramp. With six hours of any tide the water was on the slipway, and you couldn't launch any other way. (21)

You could let go of the two securing ropes and work on one halyard and the two for'ard chains – that's what we liked about it. You couldn't do them four as quick as you could do that as one. (1 and 12)

It was pulled either by the coxswain or second-coxswain who was on the deck, to release the boat. The arm drops away, and the pin is then released, allowing the boat to go forward and off the carriage. (22)

Judging the moment to launch – on to the 'flat' between the wave that has just broken and the next wave.

This launch, in October 1990, saw the departure of the *Manchester Unity of Oddfellows* at the end of her service at Sheringham.

She was replaced, briefly, by the *Lloyds II*, before the offshore boats gave way to inshore boats.

23. A 'Shout'

This is *not* a practice! In the first photograph in this sequence the lifeboat, the *Calouste Gulbenkian* (a relief boat serving while the *Manchester Unity of Oddfellows* was away being serviced), has left the lifeboat house and has been turned through 90 degrees on the turntable, and the crew and helpers are making final preparations to launch. Invariably, 'shouts' occur when the sea conditions are poor – as in this example, when a skiff from Weybourne got into difficulties.

In the foreground of the second shot is the launching-off post which supports the hauling-off warp or rope seen going to the left of the photograph, with ropes being attached from the lifeboat for'ard and aft. In rough seas, at high water, this aid was invaluable.

In the third shot the lifeboat has just left the carriage, having used the quick-release pin, and it is at this precise moment that the real value of the hauling-off rope can be seen. Off the carriage, but not yet reacting to the propellers and rudder, the lifeboat is being pushed to one side by the waves, and needs the rope to help maintain its course and clear the nearby breakwater while it gets forward momentum.

You'd have a rope for'ard and a rope aft and, as you went off, the boat had 'ringles' that went round the hauling-off rope. And, as you powered out to sea, this would keep you pointing out to sea. Once we were outside that, we'd let the ropes go. (21)

In August 1961, the *Manchester Unity of Oddfellows* received a shout to a converted ship's lifeboat, the *Lucy*. The *Lucy* fired a flare off Cley when she got into trouble in rough seas, and when the Sheringham lifeboat got alongside, the four crew were taken off, and the *Lucy* was taken in tow.

The owner's wife was suffering from severe exhaustion, and 'Downtide' West decided it was important to get her to hospital as soon as possible. The *Lucy* was cast off, eventually coming ashore at Salthouse. Meanwhile, no time was wasted in getting the exhausted sailor ashore.

A sailor from the *Lucy* seen here being carried ashore by the lifeboat crew, and being met and helped by the station's Honorary Secretary, Brigadier Kent Lemon.

Honorary Secretary

The station's Honorary Secretaries had a pivotal role in operating the lifeboats. They were the authority to launch the lifeboat, and would then have the task of liaising with other stations, Head Office and other organisations, as well as making any necessary local arrangements – such as warm clothing, food, transport, and accommodation.

24. Rockets, Maroons and Mortars

The original coastguard cottages in The Driftway, and the flagstaff on the front, are a reminder of the days when Sheringham had a sizeable presence of coastguards to try to prevent smuggling. Moreover, before lifeboats, they were the only organisation that had any role in life-saving – hence the Rocket Brigade.

By the 1860s, the coastguard service came under the Admiralty, providing a reserve for the Royal Navy. Moreover, during the First World War most coastguards were called up for active service, leaving just a skeleton force, supported by Sea-Scouts. Bill Thirtle's father came to Sheringham as one such Sea-Scout, and was billeted with one of the coastguard families.

The Coastguard Station was important in the day-to-day safety of fishing boats.

The mast was used to hoist the gale cone. It was all black leather and fixed to a rope going about three-quarters way up the mast. If the cone was hanging downwards that would mean the gale was coming off the land, and the other way up, the gale would be coming off the sea.

When the lifeboat was off, there'd have to be a man that could 'talk' to the shore with flags, and the coastguard would stand near the mast and watch the signalman send a message, using a telescope.

View from the Coastguard Station over the West Beach.

Opposite the cottages was the look-out building, facing north. Close by was a large flag-pole, and mortars – in which they placed the lifeboat maroons. A separate building contained the life-saving apparatus. This was a four-wheeled vehicle with wide-rimmed wheels for going over soft ground to the cliff-edge. It contained tripods, rockets, ropes and breeches buoy.

The Brigade consisted of several coastguards, and four or five men appointed in the town. They weren't coastguards at all, but they were interested in life-saving. One of them was Arthur Tice – a shoemaker. Two shoemakers were involved in firing the rocket. The coastguards were paid, but not the rocket crew – it was voluntary.

There were rescues 'once in a blue moon' – they could go ten years and not save anybody, but were there at the cliff-edge if needed.

The Rocket Brigade at the top of the Admiralty Slipway, with several coastguard members – and a ghostly dog!

Tom Gray and Jack Gray owned the horses used by the Brigade. They were carriers what used to carry all goods from the Railway Station. They had a tumbler and two drays, and they used to cart goods around the town.

The Brigade would practise four times a year, in front of the coastguard mast and, in summer-time, they warned people to keep back off the beach – for safety. They'd point the rocket launcher towards the Upcher breakwater [see also p. 63].

On the breakwater they used to have an upright pole – somewhere around 5 foot 6 inches above the top of the breakwater. They'd aim the rocket at that pole, and the rocket was attached to a life-saving bag what you can step in and sit down. That was made of calico with corks all on the outside, and as the rocket went, that would take this bag with the long line attached right back to the shore. They would start to pull, and the man being rescued on Upcher's breakwater would be brought 'ashore', pretending that Upcher's breakwater was a ship – the upright pole represented a mast. (9)

25. A Red Sky at Night

Every fishing community would have taken a keen interest in the weather, and made use of folklore and old sayings to try to forecast it accurately. Some of these are quite fanciful. For example:

> When the young moon's on her back
> Of fine weather there's no lack;
> But when the new moon's off her back,
> Take in sail and homeward tack.

Others, however, have more scientific substance to them. For instance: 'Rain before seven, clear by eleven' is linked to the passage of weather fronts in depressions, which seldom give more than four hours of rain.

'A red sky at night' is a fisherman's delight, as well as a shepherd's – but with the sea, it's not quite so straightforward. While the weather might change for the better quite quickly after a storm, once the sea surface is whipped up, it takes much longer for waves to moderate. Once generated, wave-forms continue until they break on a coastline, and this may be a long way from where they originated. The photograph below shows just such a situation.

There was little or no wind on this pleasant morning in May 1988, but, there was a swell and, at high water large waves were even breaking on to the road in front of the Crown Inn. The waves had been generated well to the north, and made any attempt to launch crab boats extremely hazardous, if not impossible.

Forecasting the weather, and the likely state of the sea has also always been difficult because they both can change quite suddenly. There have been numerous occasions when crab boats have gone to sea in fine weather, only for them to be grateful for the support of the lifeboat as they battled to return in foul conditions. The diary of 'Coaly' Cooper, coxswain of the *Henry Ramey Upcher* lifeboat, provides just one example of this:

October 27th, 1894 – boats out after whelks and cod fish. They went to sea in the morning when the weather was fine, but a heavy swell on the shore. The sky then started looking very bad and with the sea getting up the boats could not get home. The sea was very rough when we launched the lifeboat and we took twelve fishermen out of six boats. (23)

The 1953 storm surge resulted in damage to the promenade and cliffs – but, clearly, not the degree of damage experienced elsewhere. The *Foresters Centenary* was to be launched in the days following the floods, and it was lucky to escape serious damage.

Cromer was off, Wells was off, and we were off a little while because the turntable was blocked. We went down to the boat-house and shovelled the stones away at 3.30 a.m. At the boat-house, the verandah was all in pieces, the doors were off, the windows were gone. The 'Foresters Centenary' was pushed in the corner but didn't get damaged. All Sunday we were clearing the debris, and we got a 'shout' on the Monday. (12)

The crab boat *Enterprise* was also to suffer a similar fate after a storm in 1988. Waves breaking onto the Fishermen's Slope during a storm are funnelled by the shape of the Slope, and push boats to the top of the Slope. The bow of the *Enterprise* (see p. 79) was badly damaged as it was thrown against the wall and other boats.

Storms can also damage pots on the sea-bed particularly those that have been continuously submerged, the bows rot and are easily snapped by turbulent water.

The *Liberty* resting precariously at the top of the Fishermen's Slope, following the 1953 storm surge

Teddy 'Lux' Craske and Jacko West unloading damaged pots.

26. The Whole North Sea to Myself

Jimmy 'Paris' West –
a remarkable lifeboatman

Jimmy 'Paris' West was a remarkable man, and something of a lifeboat legend, being one of the last surviving members of the *J C Madge* crew. Even approaching his nineties he would still walk from his home 'Idunno' (his shed was called 'Nor do I'), to the promenade, 'just to see if the sea was still there'. He was, amongst other things, a first-class golfer. Jimmy's many visitors would often comment on his remarkable sense of humour, retained over the years despite the personal tragedies life had thrown at his family, as with many others in this fishing community.

After more than 60 years he remembered clearly the rescue of the *SS Ulla* of Bergen, February 1914, in the most atrocious weather. He was at the 'picture palace' when the mortars went, having just returned from Yarmouth, with a blizzard following him. The film was about a ship sinking, and when Jimmy thought he heard the mortars, his chums made fun of him. But he was right.

We went straight away from there to the lifeboat shed across the snow, across the golf links, which is a mile and a quarter – blowing a living gale. My uncle was coxswain. His name was Obadiah Cooper. He got up in the shed and he shouted out: 'Now you know boys, this is a rough bad night. Terrible night. But what are you willing to do?' he say. 'The Wells lifeboat has phoned through to Cromer and say they's unable to launch. The Cromer people ha' now phoned through to Sheringham to say they's unable to launch. That's up to you boys. What are we going to do?' Well we didn't know no better. We said we'd have a go. We plunged down into the sea. She buried herself. Well I thought I was in the water. I thought I had the whole North Sea to myself.

It took several attempts with the rope to get out as far as the anchor, and putting the mast up was very difficult, But the rescue was a success, except for the terrible anxiety for the families at home, who heard nothing for several days, and assumed the worst.

Jimmy pausing for a moment between braiding pots,
outside his house, 'Idunno', in Cliff Road.

One secret Jimmy kept until late in life was his wartime missions. This account is as told to Stanley Craske:

At the beginning of the war I was asked at a private interview if I would undertake special work and, agreeing, was then sworn to secrecy, as the work came under British Intelligence (Special Service). I would have to take my motor boat out in the middle of the night, or early hours, and lay offshore about two miles out. When I heard an aircraft engine I was to look for certain coloured lights in a pattern only I knew. I was then to watch, usually for two people, dropped into the sea by parachute and quickly pick them out and bring them ashore. They were British Secret Agents, spies to you and me, who had been working in France and Holland.

But one morning things almost ended in disaster:
To launch from the East Beach the sentries, who had been warned, made a gap in the barbed-wire defences, and assisted me to push my boat off, then waited for three flashing lights signal from me when I returned with my passengers. However, this morning the tide was stronger than I had anticipated, so I had to miss the East Beach and land opposite the Fishermen's Gangway. The sentries, of course, weren't expecting me, and thinking I might be German boats, when I flashed my light, opened up with machine guns. Luckily, when they fired at my lights, I'd come in quickly to shore, and in the darkness they'd missed me.
(20)

A splendid working photograph of Jimmy, possibly on board the *Britisher*. Other boats in his long career included the *White Heather*, with Billy Butcher and Bob 'Rally' West (lost when cut adrift), the *Englishman*, and *Miss England*.

Jimmy 'Paris'

As with so many nicknames, so with the Sheringham fishermen, origins are often obscure. One version is that Jimmy's father was hurling stones into the sea one evening and when asked what he was doing said he was 'bombing Paris'. Another version is that (perhaps as a child) he was marching round a field with a gun, apparently 'defending Paris' – in the year 1871 Paris was under siege from Prussia.

27. He Never Missed a Trip

Teddy Craske with his brother Young Billy 'Cutty' bringing their peds ashore.

Teddy 'Lux' Craske was one of the most respected of any local fisherman, always shunning publicity for himself. During the last war all lifeboat crew-members were under pressure for much of the time. Teddy's daughter Hazel remembers how the lifeboat was a central part of her father's life, and how precious sleep was to him:

Like most fishermen, Teddy worked very long hours, and on top of that he had daily lifeboat duties, running the engine and checking the turntable for wedged-in stones, for example, so no wonder he has been known to fall asleep at the table over his dinner! Sunday morning was the big cleaning day at the lifeboat shed. Henry Little and Teddy 'Fiddy' would always be in the upstairs room practising morse. They were brilliant! Teddy never missed a trip except on the few occasions the lifeboat was launched to the 'Liberty' [his own boat], when he was transferred to the lifeboat. He was the first to be called, as he fired the maroons, which he kept in his shed on the cliff. He dried the rocket line in front of our fire and we weren't allowed to breathe near it when it had been woven on to its frame. (6)

Teddy 'Lux' Craske (right) fitting a set of 'crinnies' or 'spouts' (the central tunnel) to his pots, with brother Billy 'Cutty' (left) and father, Old Billy 'Cutty', in their shed at the top of The Driftway. The photo was taken in the 1950s.

Teddy Craske with Henry 'Downtide' West, on board the *Foresters Centenary*. Teddy is preparing to fire the rocket line, which was an essential piece of equipment. The line was wound carefully on to a frame, and when fired across to a ship in distress would enable the 'breeches buoy' to be used. This photograph, taken about 1960, may have been on the last Lifeboat Day for the *Foresters Centenary*.

Picture by Eastern Daily Press, Norwich

Teddy served in all four restored lifeboats, and he and 'Downtide' West received medals for their part in the *Wimbledon* rescue. This is how it was reported:

Motor mechanic Craske was at times up to his armpits in water at the engine controls and had to hold the radio telephone above his head. For the rescue of the last three survivors the coxswain and motor mechanic had to work in exact unison and only by great skill was severe damage prevented when the lifeboat was almost carried on to the steamer. Mr Craske would only make this comment. 'It was not a very nice trip.' (24)

There was one amusing incident that Henry West remembered, when the poor old *Foresters Centenary* was struggling to get away in a heavy sea:

She'd took one or two and she actually come astern. 'Downtide' was coxswain then, and all of a sudden he said to Teddy, on the throttle, 'Go on, Teddy, give it the lot!' 'Give it the lot,' he said, 'she's had the lot since we shoved off.' (1)

Teddy had two brothers: Jack, the younger, was sadly lost at sea (see p. 82) and his other brother, Billy 'Cutty' Jr., also died at sea, though in a quite different way, aged 72:

There was a bit of a swell and Teddy pushed off with other fishermen dithering. Billy shouted, 'Come on, it's lovely! However, in that trip, Billy said he was thirsty, offered Teddy a piece of orange and slid down the boat. What a way to go, still doing what he loved. I was devastated, and as for Dad, well, they were joined at the hip. (6)

28. Who Likes Coshies?

Visitors to Sheringham asked to be introduced to 'Go-father' Pegg, and a whole generation in Sheringham remembers his 'spider song'.

It is often lamented that the world is poorer for its lack of 'characters'. It is perhaps difficult to define what the term means, but there are few that knew 'Go-father' Pegg who would hesitate to include him. Photos show him surrounded by children. In later years he earned his money by deck-chairs and tents, and in using his small boat for trips:

There was several skiffs, doing nothing else only taking people out. 'Go-father's was one in particular. He was an East Ender but he used to land to do most of his 'pleasuring' on the West. When he had finished his last lot, all us boys, and girls too, we'd all know what was going to happen with 'Go-father'. He used to git us all into his boat and we'd row him to the East End. He'd sit up the stern on 'er, and as we was rowing we'd have to sing his war song:

> *Look upon the wall.*
> *You'll see a great spider,*
> *Glory to his great long legs,*
> *Wibbledy, Wobbledy,*
> *Hit him on the nobbledy,*
> *Then there'll be no more cobwebs.*

When we got off at the East End – if there was plenty of sand – he'd pull two great old handfuls of toffees out of his pocket. 'Who likes coshies?' And he'd chuck them over the sand. Of course we'd all scrap for 'em. Well after that we had to pull him up the beach. (25)

He obviously needed bulk purchases of these Callard and Bowser toffees, but rather than buy them direct, he bought them from the Army and Navy Stores in Victoria Street, London, because he had shares in it. 'Go-father' naturally became somewhat of a celebrity for holiday-makers. When they arrived, they would ask to be directed to him, and his red hat and white beard would mark him out. But one particular Londoner met more than his match when he tried to score a point or two from the old man, saying he could not understand why 'Go-father' stayed in Sheringham, when there was so much money to be made in London.

'Go-father' let him have his say, then he said: 'Well look here, my man. You are having full board at my house, aren't you?' 'That's correct.' 'You're paying full board money for your wife and two children for a fortnight?' 'That's correct.' 'I take you fishing in my boat, don't I?' 'Yes.' 'And you pay me, don't you?' 'Yes, I do.' 'I'm learning your children to swim, aren't I?' 'That's correct.' 'And you're paying, aren't you?' 'I am.' 'You have a tent off me on the beach, don't you?' 'That's right.' 'And you're paying, aren't you?' 'That's correct.' 'Now my man,' 'Go-father' said, 'you in London have to work 50 weeks in the year and put your money one side to come here for a fortnight. And you want me to go up there and do the same!' With that the Londoner walked away with his head down. (12)

Skiffs would use sails and oars, and in this lovely photograph of an early beach scene, 'Go-father' is, as always, surrounded by children.

'Go-father' (Go-farther)
'Go-father's nickname apparently came about in a fairly mundane way, considering the numerous stories about the old man. He apparently had the habit of saying: 'If you want to earn a living, you've got to go farther.' It was assumed he meant, 'you've got to fish farther out than the others'. But in the light of his astuteness in business, and in predicting how Sheringham would develop, there may have been more to the remark than simply fishing!

29. I Go a-Fishing

A famous portrait of Willie Long by Olive Edis. With a sailcloth around his shoulders, the photographer has captured the spirit of this remarkable man.

There was a strong religious tradition within Sheringham's fishing community, especially embracing the Salvation Army and Methodism. Sundays were very strict. Fishermen would put their boots on after midnight, and children were expected to attend church or chapel:

My grandfather was strict Methodist. I went to chapel three times on a Sunday, Sunday School included. The evening was the highlight. There would be fishermen preaching. One of 'em was the famous Willie Long. I remember one time his text was 'I go a-fishing' and that one really was a good un. We used to sit there pumping the organ, watching this bit of lead going up and down. Then for the sermon, when Willie was going to preach, or anyone, we'd come into the chapel. (1)

Other Fishermen evangelists included John 'Teapot' West, James Middleton, and 'Tonny Dingy' Craske, who was famed for his singing:

He was a big man with a voice rich and resonant. One of his favourite hymns was 'take off the old coat, put on the new'. Often when he warmed to his work Tonny would suit the action to the words and strip off his jacket and reveal his blue fisherman's jersey beneath. Often I have accompanied Tonny Craske in his pony and trap to the village chapels and have been thrilled to see how joyously the country folk have received him as an old friend. On these excursions there was always the pleasant ritual of feeding the pony and lighting lanterns before we came home. (26)

The Salvation Army in Sheringham probably started from the Grimsby fishing connection:

The Grimsby Salvation Army more or less converted all these in their way, and the fishermen said, 'when we git back to Sheringham we'll start one up. This look a good thing'. They started in the old net loft, where Cally Emery used to build the boats. Old Harry Grice,who lived at Weybourne, he started a band going. Then they moved into Cremer Street. (12)

'Teapot' West

Nicknames in Sheringham were usually passed down in families, and almost anything that happened to a fisherman could lead to a nickname. Lenny 'Teapot' West's grandfather John was responsible for his nickname. It seems that in the days of the Royal Flying Corps, an airman's plane ditched off Cromer, and John West was responsible for saving his life. The airman's wife, to show her immense gratitude for this act, presented Lenny's grandmother with a silver teapot, which of course the family still possesses.

One of the highlights of the Salvation Army in later years was the 'Harvest of the Sea'.

'Downtide' West, he started that off just after the war, following the service for Scottish visitors. We'd spend a week decorating the hall up, and then Mollie, his daughter, she used to get every boat's name that was fishing, and in the nets you'd put all these. During the service we always blessed the fish. The fishermen would come in, and they all had a plate each, with four or five bits of cod, or salmon, crabs, sprats, anything what's caught. They'd all bring it and put it at the front on a long table. And then whoever was doing the meeting he got the Lord to bless that, and for the safe return of the fishermen. (12)

'Tonny Dingy' Craske with his wife Gertrude. Tonny would visit the outlying chapels in his cart, and return by the light of the carriage lamps.

The Salvation Army citadel would be bulging at the seams for this popular service. Many familiar fishermen are seen in this photograph, together with Major and Mrs Major Downs.

30. Back on the Beach

Bob Rushmer, Fishery Officer for North Norfolk, in characteristic pose.
He enjoyed working amongst his fishermen friends.

Bob Rushmer applied for the position of Fishery Officer in 1952, having first taken advice from his dear old father:

In his 'bootiful Norfolk', he said: 'now do yew look hare ol' pardner, if yew ken git thet job, then dew yew hev it.' That was all I needed to hear. I went over to King's Lynn for an interview and was offered the job. I then began what was to become one of the most fulfilling periods in my life. While I was not exactly at sea, at least I was back on the beach in my new role as Fishery Officer for the North Norfolk Region. This region stretched from Hunstanton to Great Yarmouth which must be one of the most beautiful areas on earth.

My main role was basically to prevent the catching and landing of undersized or prohibited fish and shellfish. To give a few examples of prohibited fish, these would include sea-trout or sea-salmon and undersized crabs, or say a lobster in berry [ready to give birth]. *These rules were, of course, just basic common sense; if everybody just caught undersized crabs then the species would soon disappear, as today's small crab grows into tomorrow's large crab. We used to have metal gauges, but after a few years of fishing it can just as easily be done by eye. I certainly never had any real trouble with fishermen landing undersized crabs. I never forgot that my father was a fisherman and I like to think that they could see why I had to do the job I was doing. I do recall one old fisherman in Wells, though, who I had been observing all night, who threatened to black both my eyes! For several years during the 1950s I used to start up the engines on the old lifeboat the 'Foresters Centenary', when the mechanic, Teddy Craske, was unavailable. She was a lovely old boat, she was. I even got the chance to go out in her a couple of times.*

My Number Two all of these years was Kitchener Pegg and, very often, we used to be on duty together, day and night. We used to have some laughs. I remember once when we had spent half the night watching a mysterious boat out at sea. I turned to Kitchener and said, 'Well you know what that boat is, that's the boiler light from that old ship what sunk just there a few years ago.' He just looked at me dumbfounded as I chuckled away. (27)

Kitchener Pegg (a Christian name rather than a nickname) was Bob Rushmer's Number Two, and briefly took over from him for a short period before his untimely death. He is shown here with his daughter, Penny Jewkes, who performed regularly on television in 'The Black and White Minstrel Show'.

31. Stones, Coal and Sprouts

Coal-carting was a winter occupation for some fishermen and a wartime one for some lifeboatmen.

During the hard winter months, or when the fishing was bad, anything to bring in extra money was a help. As well as tents and deck-chairs during the summer, coal-carting, forestry work, and even sprout-picking might be tackled. But a regular source of income either side of the last war was stone-picking, a job that could be strenuous and badly paid.

For the fishermen who didn't go to sea, stone-picking was very, very handy, though that was hard work. You might have injured yourself. They were a special stone in Sheringham, they are a blue stone. They are grey when they are dry and they are bluey-grey when they are wet. They musn't have too many marks on them. Size didn't matter so much but they had to be a good stone, because when you weighed-in they were examined. You picked them up on the beach in the peds, special peds for the job. If there was a neighbour near you, you'd give him a lift up on your shoulder. I've seen some people go up with their knees bent, doubled up, and struggling. The weigh-in was always at the West End but we picked where we liked.

You got 6/6d. a ton. You might pick a ton; a lot of times you didn't, so you earnt less than six bob a day. And that was really bitterly cold and you didn't have any finger-nails. (1)

Many fishermen, especially in their later years, would have a few beach huts and deck-chairs for hire. The square tents replaced the old bell tents.

During the last war, lifeboatmen would, of course, be constantly on the alert for a call-out, and the Sheringham lifeboat of this period was probably as busy as any around our coasts. But they also helped the war effort by tackling necessary jobs vacated by men serving in the forces, such as coal-carting and forestry, as Madge Gaff recalls:

My father went crabbing and then in the winter-time he went into Upcher's wood and done forestry work. He also went stone-picking, and then during the war, of course, he was with the lifeboat, so he went into the coal-yard. Several years he went into the woods, and I believe my grandad used to do that as well, years ago, work for Upcher in the woods, forestry, planting trees. He also went with a lot of the fishermen at that time sprout-picking, at Syderstone. (28)

Picture by the Eastern Daily Press, Norwich

Stone-picking was a valuable source of income either side of the war. In this Press photograph Billy 'Butterballs' Grice is seen filling plastic buckets with the blue flints that were sought after by the Stoke-on-Trent potteries. In earlier years, special peds were used for collecting the stones. They were piled as high as a house, all along the side of the Grand Hotel Leas, before being taken by rail to Stoke.

32. Apartments, Trips and Bathing-boats

The women of the families might earn a little by gansey-knitting (probably only 4/- to 9/- for all the hours of work) or would perhaps take in washing. A few men in earlier years might offer to man the 'bathing-boat', keeping an eye on the swimmers. The occasional joker might even try bottled sea-water as a cure-all for gullible Londoners. There were also trips out to sea. But the activity that most affected the whole family, was letting rooms during the season:

They all let rooms. My grandmother had Robert Morley. He gave Granny ten shillings a week. When Geoffrey Keene first went into the repertory company, at the Arcade Lawn, he took his first steps on Granny's kitchen floor. Macfarlanes biscuit people used to stay here and used to send Granny a hamper every Christmas. Granny had all these young lads come – Children's Special Service Mission – all these College boys, and when she used to take the dinner in, they'd get their knees underneath the table and lift it up. They'd all go 'hurray'. Some of 'em used to climb up and get in the bedroom window. Where they let the rooms then the people would bring the food in; you'd cook it for them and serve it to them. They used to call that 'apartments'. And there weren't many bathrooms. They had wash-stands and had these big jugs and bowls to take the water up. That was hard work. (28)

Belle Vue in Beeston Road, run by Charles and Emma Bouttell, was just one of many apartment-houses which provided accommodation for visitors to Sheringham.

A minor source of income for a few fishermen was the provision of a 'bathing-boat'. There were usually two off the East End and one off the West. These acted as a support to swimmers. The boats would be provided by the fishermen and anchored off the end of the breakwaters. 'Pepper' Wilson was one such 'bathing-boatman', and Jimmy Hannah another. They also dumped the contents of the promenade rubbish baskets out to sea!

Bathing-boats supported swimmers who might get into difficulties in the dangerous currents, or who simply needed a 'breather'.

Even before the last war, a room might bring in 30/- a week in August, and some landladies even added a cruet charge for the use of the salt and pepper! The same families might come year after year perhaps taking rooms for a month at a time, with friends staying elsewhere during the same period. But the chaos of clearing the rooms and finding somewhere else to sleep for the summer months certainly put a strain on family life:

Father never liked them coming, but he made 'em ever so welcome when they got there. And they would love to come into the living room and listen to all his yarns, about Shuck [the black ghost hound of North Norfolk] *and things. But that was a nightmare really, because you had to clear everything out of that bedroom, apart from the furniture. My father bought a very large brand new shed, which went down the bottom of the garden. That was a £1. That was a wonderful shed and so mother and father they painted it all out and put curtains up; there were two little windows. And then my brother and father slept down there.* (3)

Visitors' Books

The Belle Vue visitors' book for April 1927 contained this entry:

My mother and friend, as a means to an end
Have appointed me scribe for the lot
And I'm forced now to say, that my 'only way'
Is to talk of the weather and 'pot'
By the 'pot' I mean food and, without being rude,
Henceforth I shall call it the 'grub'.
Both the grub and the weather (we'll take 'em together)
The Devil himself couldn't snub.
The Promenade's grand and (though minus a band)
Yet its 'turns' and its 'twists' are the same.
There are no saxophones (only crab pots and bones)
For smells from the matter – no name.
The girls with their brogue and the latest of vogue,
Are a credit to any resort.
Now I cannot say more to bring people galore
To a place which could never be bought. (29)

Corporal Grice and Jimmy 'Paris' with an enthusiastic boatload of trippers. The lady with the white collar is a schoolteacher, Elizabeth Langton.

The canvas tents were on the stones and usually had ropes attached, so they could be hoisted up and suspended from the promenade railings in rough weather. Sometimes these tents would be stored inside the house during the off-season, causing considerable disruption.

In the summer months my grandfather had beach huts at the East End. There were families, the Storeys and the Emerys and the 'Chicken' Grices on the East End, the Dumbles and the Scotters on the West End. They all had several huts because they were three or four tiers deep, on the West End especially. The wooden ones were on the top. My grandfather had canvas ones as well as wooden ones. The canvas ones we kept in the house in Beeston Road, in the middle room. Someone would come and take the window out. (1)

33. Dominoes and Greasy Poles

In these early days, before the coming of television, entertainments were home-made. Many fishermen loved to sing, and there was a fishermen's choir in late Victorian times. Fiddles, accordions and step-dancing would also grace the pubs, and magic-lantern slides might be shown at the Salvation Army and elsewhere. And there was always the visiting circus and the annual regatta. In the slow winter months the fishermen would perhaps pass the hours in one or two regular meeting places.

They used to get in 'Dipper' Johnson's shoemaker's shop, for a game of cards or dominoes, or yarning. You couldn't move. You couldn't open the door without knocking somebody because the door used to open inwards. That'd be packed that solid, and you'd just be able to shove the door open so you could perhaps squeeze round as well. And when you just opened that door the smoke came out there, you'd think the whole place was on fire. (13)

It is surprising what you might find swimming in the sea along Sheringham's beaches. What a delight it must have been for local children when a circus performing on Beeston Common decided to take an elephant for a dip.

Helen Richardson describes in her diary for August 1888 how:

We went to the entertainment at the Lobster after supper, which was quite one of the most amusing I have ever been at. The fishermen's band played to us most frightfully out of tune, a fisherman sang to us, and Mr Grimes danced a hornpipe which was quite wonderful. Mr Grimes was the most amusing person there, the way he danced Sir Roger kept us in fits. (30)

The regattas, despite their popularity over a number of years (everyone around at that time remembers the 'greasy pole'), did not produce many photographs. This rare photograph shows a crab-boat race, with the *Henry Ramey* standing off.

The highlight of the summer months was the annual regatta, which brought people into Sheringham from far and wide. *That took the whole day. Yachts came from Blakeney, Morston, all over the place. The beach would be full because they'd have two or three special races for different classes of yachts. They would have motor-boat races and crab-boat-sailing races, just the old crab boat with the lug-sail. They'd have shovel races in crab boats where, instead of using oars you'd use shovels. They'd have the 'Ramey' lifeboat off and strap a great pole along her with a box on the end, with a pig in, and they'd grease the whole pole. You had to walk from the lifeboat down the pole, pull the handle and let the pig out. The pig was yours if you could do it. Johnny Broughton, he was pretty good at it.*

In the evening you'd go up on the Leas and there'd be the tug o' war between fishermen and firemen, and the firemen used to come with their great hobnail boots on. They'd dig a great hole and git into it, but they never could pull the fishermen over! They won every year. There would be boxing. They'd have a boxing ring, 'cause there was boxers in the town then. You'd have the boxing match, then to finish off you had fireworks. (13)

The final boxing bout would usually be between two of Benny Smith's young children, who would fight in gloves the size of tea-cosies, and who would be rewarded with a shower of pennies thrown into the ring! (31)

A fishermen's team in the Regatta tug o' war competition – which they always won. Hauling pots gave them something of an advantage!

Part of the Sheringham Regatta programme for Wednesday 5th August 1936 reads as follows:

The following events will take place after Nos 1 to 10 are completed:-
SHOVEL RACE   GREASED POLE
TUG-OF-WAR   Teams of Eight
Sheringham Fishermen Challenge All Comers
Will Visitors please arrange Teams
(Eight Special Prizes given by E.W. Meyerstein Esq.)
The "HENRY RAMEY UPCHER" Lifeboat
Will be Launched in the Morning and Passengers will be taken aboard
for Trips Adults 1/- Children under 14 - 6d.

34. Return of the Lifeboats

Tony Sadler was involved from the very start with attempts to get a lifeboat for the newly formed Museum.

I had heard that the 'J C Madge' used to spend the summers down at Brancaster and, being one of Sheringham's old lifeboats, I felt wouldn't that be wonderful to use her in the RNLI Lifeboat Day at Sheringham. The owner agreed, and he brought the boat down for our Lifeboat Day. So, that's how the 'J C Madge' came into the picture.

Later, the owner indicated that he was going to sell her. He also had a feeling that she ought to come back to Sheringham. The following year, she was put up for sale, and the owner let us know. We got enough money together, with the help of a local businessman who very kindly lent us the money so that we didn't lose her. And that was the start of it all.

RNLI Lifeboat Day, 1989, with the *Manchester Unity of Oddfellows* in the foreground, and the *J C Madge* in the background, as a Sea King from RAF Coltishall joins in the exercise.

In March 1989 we brought her from Lincoln to Boston, then out into the Wash and across to Brancaster. We then sailed her to Lowestoft, and into the International Boat-Building Training Centre, who did £25,000 of work on her, before we brought her home.

Having obtained the 'J C Madge', it came to our knowledge that the 'Manchester Unity of Oddfellows' was going to be brought out of service, and I was determined that, somehow, we kept her.

Eventually, the society was persuaded to obtain her for us, and they paid £500, having bought her originally, and presented her to the town.

I did a couple of articles on our collection, and I mentioned the fact it would be nice to get the 'full set', never ever dreaming that we would find her – the 'Foresters Centenary'. But, Henry 'Joyful' West and his son, through the help of the lifeboat enthusiasts, discovered her down at Burnham-on-Crouch and, would you believe, she was for sale. Virtually overnight, the Preservation Society, the Sheringham Shantymen, the Science Museum and various people made contributions, allowing us to buy her. So, we've got the 'full set': we've got over 100 years of Sheringham lifeboats.

As a member of the Sheringham Shantymen, I said it would be rather a nice idea if we had got a bit of money left over (after money was given to charity), to give it to the Museum Trust. I then changed that request, suggesting we bought materials for the renovation of the lifeboats. I changed it again – I said, 'let us give some money, let's buy the materials, but, let's go and use them' – in other words, 'let's put the paint on the boats; let's form a team for renovation and restoration of these lovely old boats'. (32)

Work under way on the deck of the *Foresters Centenary*. The cabin, or 'cuddy', was in a Cromer garden for seventeen years but, originally, had been on a Caister lifeboat.

The Sheringham Shantymen in front of the *Henry Ramey Upcher* lifeboat shed.

35. Return of the Fishing Boats

Tony Sadler recalls:

I got a phone call one day from a boat-yard down at Burnham Overy. 'Are you interested in an old Sheringham crab boat?' 'Yes,' I said, 'of course.' They said, 'Right, we'll pass it on to the owner that you'd like her.' It was the 'Mollie Florence', which was old 'Downtide's crab boat. A crowd of us got a towing-vehicle and a carriage, and we went and picked her up, and she was like a piece of jelly. There were no guts at all, ribs had gone and timbers were rotten, the stern-post dropped out.

We taught ourselves to steam ribs, and the National Trust got us some timber which was lovely and we made up a steam box, and we waved our magic wand! That was the start of the collection of crab boats. (32)

The *Mollie Florence* was kept in storage in a National Trust barn at Upper Sheringham. In this photograph, the boat, only partially restored, provided a photo opportunity for the Sheringham Shantymen – many of whom have helped in moving boats, as well as restoration work.

Pictured from left to right are: Keith Zeland of the National Trust, Bill Thirtle, Peter Page, Tony Sadler, Mary Blythe (Museum President), Mike Hill, Hugh Arbuthnot, Billy Branch, and Henry 'Joyful' West, with Eddie Bailey in the foreground.

Picture by the Eastern Daily Press, Norwich

Sid 'Plug' Emery is seen here with the *Enterprise*, built by his father, and with his friend Henry West.

Another fishing boat in the Museum Collection is the *Enterprise*, which was laid down for 'Plug' Emery at the start of World War II. He was then called up, spending the war in the Royal Navy.

When he wrote home, he always asked about progress on the boat. In fact, there was none, as the business had other work to do. It was only at the end of the War, just before 'Plug' was due home, that work really started – so the *Enterprise* was ready when he returned home.

The next one was the 'Enterprise'. Nicky Knights had found the 'Enterprise', 'Plug' Emery's old boat, down somewhere in Essex. Again, it had been used as a pleasure craft, and he went off and bought this to bring home and restore and use it. Unfortunately, it had an accident on the Slipway (the bow was smashed in during a winter storm). He rang me up one day and said, 'Tony, would you like the "Enterprise"?' Of course, I said, 'Yes.' We took her up to Hall Farm, Upper Sheringham. She's been restored now. Billy Thirtle has done a tremendous amount of work on her; he was the leading light on that, although we all mucked in, of course.

And then, poor old Arthur Scotter left us, and when the 'Windsor Rose' came out of the water, she was put into storage at Blakeney, and Peter Scotter said he'd like the Museum to look after her. And it was agreed that we'd take charge of the old boat. So, we've got her in the Museum collection as well.

But, we've got another one as well because, we've got the 'QJ & J'. Somebody rang us up from Essex somewhere, and said they'd got the old 'QJ & J' – Henry Blogg's old crab boat – again, built in Sheringham. Peter Brooks said to me, 'Do we want it? If not, they're going to put a chain-saw into it.' And so the 'QJ & J' has come to Sheringham as well. We've got a lot of work to do on that and the plans are not completely set on what we're going to do. But I think she's going to be dropped into a steel cradle somehow, and I'd like to see her stand outside the Oddfellows Hall as a memorial to the crab boats that followed. She would stand within a few metres of where she was built by the Emerys. (32)

New strakes were riveted into the damaged bow section of the *Enterprise* while in storage at Aylsham. Supports were used to keep the boat's shape during this delicate work, until the missing ribs and bits were replaced. Here, Bill Thirtle is seen checking detail, before the final strake was fitted.

Strakes, ribs and bits

Strakes are the horizontal timbers providing the outside facing of a boat, and are secured to the ribs – narrow, vertical timbers inside the boat which help give it rigidity. Further strength is provided by the thwarts – the seats – and the bits. These are positioned just in front of the bow and the stern, and are seemingly insignificant pieces of timber, but they lock everything into place.

36. The Continuing Lifeboat Story

The change-over from *Atlantic 21* (left) to *Atlantic 75* (right) in front of the lifeboat house.

It came as a shock when the RNLI decided not to have a large boat replacement for the 'Manchester Unity'. We tried our best to get them to replace it with an offshore boat. Unfortunately, the case wasn't strong enough, and they needed a fast-response boat somewhere on this stretch of coastline. So, with both Cromer and Wells, either side of us, being earmarked for a faster offshore boat, the obvious place as far as the RNLI was concerned was the one in between.

A big change at the time from offshore to inshore was the age difference – anyone over 45 wasn't going to be allowed on the new boat – so, we lost good lifeboatmen. And then we had to train for a completely different type of boat, one which would attack the sea, instead of riding it. The Oakley-class did a maximum of about eight knots to a fast-response boat doing anything between 30 to 35 knots. The lower age limit was related to the pounding the body took at high speeds.

The first boat we got was the Atlantic 21. That arrived as a relief boat because the next class was being developed and we were earmarked for one of those. The crew had to learn a completely different concept of lifeboat work. While there were several trained helmsmen, it was always the first trained helmsman who arrived, and the next two crew-members, helmsmen or not, would make up the crew of three. The fastest there were the crew. The average time for an Atlantic-class launch at Sheringham is between six and seven minutes; the Oakley was about fifteen minutes. (21)

The *Atlantic 75*, a fast-response boat, 'attacking' the sea off Blakeney.

When we got the 'Atlantic 75', it was slightly wider, with bigger engines – a better boat. It was bought by the Manchester Unity of Oddfellows, keeping the association with this society. (21)

A typical launch for the *Atlantic 75* – its tractor reversing into the water, allowing her to float and leave the cradle.

37. A Dangerous Job

Eric Wink

Jack Craske

Whether in a crab boat or a lifeboat, the job had its dangers. When conditions were bad, it would be an anxious wait for wives and children until the boats returned. Below are just a few examples of close calls and some of the lesser dangers of fishing – even the seemingly ordinary task of working crab pots.

When you had all your pots in the boat at once, you had to know how you stacked them and the order you put them in, and they had to come out in that order. If you're steaming along, and you throw the wrong pot out, the tow is going to get tight and snarl up the other tows in the boat and there's four or five pots coming at you if you don't look out! It's dangerous with the anchor as well. If you get the anchor snarled up, that will come for'ard like a rocket. You can't get out of the way of them because there's nowhere to go to get out of the way. (13)

Eric Wink was a good fisherman and a good seaman. An anchor caught in his oilskin and he went over the side. A crew-member had the common sense to grab hold of the dan [a buoy] *right near the boat to make the boat fast. Eric went down and he said this anchor had caught in his oilskin, and he kept shaking and shaking and he couldn't get it off. He said, 'I looked up and saw my cap floating up to the surface. I struggled, and in the end I gave up, thinking this was "it", this is how I'm supposed to go. I relaxed, and you wouldn't believe it, but the anchor dropped away.' He was wearing seaboots and he came up to the bow and they grabbed him and pulled him round to the stern. He put his foot on the bar just below the propeller, and they pulled him out. He hurt his ribs and what not. But he went back to sea.* (32)

In February 1931, Teddy Craske lost his brother, Jack:
They called the Cromer boat out. You see, we were just a pulling boat, and it needed a motor boat in them great seas. We rowed towards Jack, and his boat came towards us – but then it just went under – must've been full of water. Jack Davies of the Cromer boat, jumped in after Jack – he got a silver medal for that. But Jack went under the bows of the Cromer boat. They got hold of his hair, but they couldn't get hold properly, and he just went. (33)

The Belfast 'barker' engine could also spell danger: *They were just like a cylinder with a massive flywheel. You had to pull the brass starting-handle, and the flywheel was going round against your feet all day long. Where I used to stand would be about five to twelve inches from this great flywheel going round.* (13)
Even starting it could be perilous: *It took some turning over and how they didn't break their wrists, I don't know. Broken fingers were common, because of kickback. They were all patched up, what had them engines.* (12)

The *Windsor Rose* leaving the beach and going through the surf. This surf zone, just off the beach, could provide the most dangerous moments of any trip – particularly the launch.